Berries, Tickles and Saltwater Ice

REG FAUST

The Holy Bible: Authorized King James Version *(Translation). Psalms 4:8; 55:20-21; Song of Solomon 8:5a, 6-7.* Oxford University Press, London, UK., 1911.

Produced by:

FriesenPress

Suite 300 – 852 Fort Street
Victoria, BC, Canada V8W 1H8

www.friesenpress.com

Distributed to the trade by The Ingram Book Company

Acknowledgements

I would like to dedicate this story to Kim Courtney, Elizabeth Durnford and the people of Francois, Newfoundland for their courage, their faith, and sense of genuine community.

I would like to express my very deep gratitude to my wife, Mary Jane and friend Debbie Lindsay who have been closely involved on this project with me every step of the way; to my readers Gladina Talarico of Virgin Arm, NL; Dale Wells of St. Anthony, NL; all have given me their unconditional support and helpful criticisms during the writing of this book.

Elizabeth Balogh is certainly an editor of admirable patience, and possesses a remarkable attention to detail. Thank you.

I would also like to thank David and Barbara Adams, Jim and Sophie Bessie of Tickle Inn, Cape Onion on the north shore of the Rock for their ever generous hospitality, and enthusiasm to share with us all Newfoundland's incomparable life, stories and songs.

A very special note of gratitude goes to Earl B. Pilgrim, friend, and Newfoundland's consummate storyteller. Whether we were born on the Rock, or have become a "*Newfoundlander-by-Choice*," whether we live here or elsewhere, Earl has championed our story, kept us in touch with our roots and made us very proud to be who we are, Newfoundlanders.

I am "somewhere" present in most every "story" whether as a physician sitting on the banks of Conche Bay, Labrador, a pilot, the outport nurse, as part of the family struggling with the death of their child, or just "someone" in a group of Newfoundlanders. The times have been altered, the names all changed.

Cover photograph:Blue Cove Sunset Northern Peninsula Newfoundland and other photographs courtesy of Dennis Minty Nature Photography (http://thehumannaturecompany.ca), P.O. Box 703, Clarke's Beach, Newfoundland, Canada, A0A 1W0.

Introduction

From off the banks of the St. Lawrence River in Kingston, Ontario, the story moves along to a small island along the eastern shores of the Labrador Sea, separated from the mainland by a shallow tickle whose waters rise and fall with the ebb and flow of tides. When the tide is in, the people who live on this island, cross by zodiac, rowboat, even kayak; when it is out, they drive across in their pickups.

As their forebears before them, these Newfoundlanders live on the edge of the sea where the Straits of Belle Isle meet the Labrador Sea, along that sea as far north to the foot of the Torngat Mountains, and southwest to St. Anthony, a sea that they have come to know intimately, a sea that gives and takes, bestows her gifts yet at times brings with her gut-wrenching loss and heartache.

This is a story of a group of people who leave the glaring lights and comforts of the city and move to this windswept land of austere beauty. Here in quietness and exposure, most, but not all, experience peace and healing in their disquieted lives, and learn from Newfoundlanders and Inuit, deep-felt values that impact them significantly.

In some sense, it is a story of exile and homecoming. This idea grew out of a set of "stories" that soon became a tapestry of many colours, some bright, while others dark. Knitted together in the twine loft of my memory and imagination, this "story" reflects my own impressions and reminiscences of the time I once lived and worked on the coast. I came to love these Newfoundlanders, who reached out to teach me and I grew; they accepted me, and I in return found my home among them.

—Reg Faust, Cape Onion, Newfoundland

Berries, Tickles and Saltwater Ice

I was very impressed with this book. *BERRIES, TICKLES AND SALTWATER ICE* by Reg Faust is so descriptive in its nature that it touches on the visual and has the ability to place you into each situation with a realistic sense of being there. The characters are true to life, touching your heart with a powerful sense of honesty and reality.

As you travel with him, Faust creates an actual experience for the readers, transporting them to a land where nature plays the part of master and isolation is an absolute. Faust combines a love of the land with love for the people in this work.

This story will carry you to the cold north, and at the same time the stories of truth and fortitude warm one's heart. It shows us that life on the edge is always precarious and nothing should ever be taken for granted. Rather love of the land, people and work can carry life lessons that will sustain you forever – and the title, as with the story, has a sense of Newfoundland flair with it, a uniqueness that is *ours*.

Kim Courtney, Former Mayor, Francois, Newfoundland South Shore

It has been my joy and privilege to have known Reg Faust and his family for many years. His gift of coming alongside people and their life situations is one which carried him well in his time with us. As many residents of northern Newfoundland and coastal Labrador communities will attest, the outport nurses and medical teams were a lifeline to the people who lived there. The inspiration and example of Dr. Wilfred Grenfell and people like Nurse Bennett caught fire in their hearts, and their mission carried on in spite of severe weather, physical hardships, limited financial resources, and sometimes, unpredictable modes of transportation. The success of their efforts was also significantly dependent on positive and strong team bonding. Each one was vitally important to the other. While this collection of remembrances encompasses the people of the outports, it is also the story of the life of the nurses as people with their own struggles and victories.

The people of this area are survivors, and they lived a life that needs to be remembered not only by them, but by their children, grandchildren, and those privileged enough to live close to them. Knowing their stories of insight and bold courage helps us to understand and better appreciate their experience.

In this collection of stories from his own time in our communities, Reg has been able to provide us with a unique view into the lives and interactions of the people. In addition, as a master weaver, he blends the circumstances of their existence into a colourful tapestry of character interactions and personal fortitude. Each story is gripping in its own way, and will give every reader yet another piece of the special life we live in this glorious land called Newfoundland and Labrador.

Dale Wells, Heritage Presenter
L'Anse aux Meadows National Historic Site,
Newfoundland

I

Big Sea, Green Point, Newfoundland

For a long while in the cool of that early October morning Philip Patey sat alone on a bench near the shore of the St. Lawrence - reading. Most often, however, he merely gazed across the river, wistful for home.

Three years before he had left his family on the east Labrador coast to attend Queen's University for graduate studies. Today, more than ever, he felt a longing homesickness for the land on which he spent most of his life, for the bergy-bits that drift into the bay, for the moose family that graze in the small pasture behind the house, and for the puffin colony that nests in the eastern cliffs high along the water's edge.

This is where his father taught him to fish and to live off the land. At home early mornings were already filled with the aroma of fresh bread being baked, and the smells of the sea quickened him as he walked to school. Now all this memory stirred him.

In particular Philip remembered his last afternoon before leaving for the mainland.

Walking along the landwash off Cape Onion, he sat down to rest. Ahead of him across the bay lay the Sacred Islands and to his left a grounded iceberg, and beyond the lighthouse on Quirpon Island.

The fog came in from the southeast advancing towards him with a soft refreshing breeze from off the sea. It slowly engulfed the lighthouse, then the grounded iceberg, rolling and drifting over the islands until they too became blanketed from view. Philip decided to wait and to feel himself inundated. An unexpected excitement had begun within him when suddenly the fog stayed, then suddenly began to roll back and unfold. As it did, rays of the mid-afternoon sun streamed over his left shoulder and onto the Great Sacred Island in the foreground and exposing the bright aqua hues of the stranded iceberg. The lesser islands could be seen only in hazy outline.

He looked on in amazement as layers of colours, orange, green, azure lay across the lee side of the island, shimmering and caressing over the volcanic bare, black rock of the land. The pattern of colours stood there for what seemed to Philip a very long time.

Suddenly, they faded and the thin layer of fog previously left behind, receded.

There remained the islands standing silent and immoveable as if forever untouched, and here below the shale ledge on which Philip sat, the plentiful, adorned and often alien rocks moved beneath the shallow waters of the shore, having come here to the Cape from immeasurable deeps, and through countless thousand millennia.

Moving away from the rocky landwash, he began to climb the path towards the summit of those hills that would bring him in view of the Labrador. Though the climb had grown steep Philip never lost sight of the white pine and black spruce lining the path, clumped close together, their crowns straining towards the light, their trunks left brittle in the darkened forest floor. Nevertheless, ascending past this dense foliage, he emerged into the clearing where the sea began to open up ahead of him. Blue Flag Irises by the hundreds, tiny, pink evergreen shrubs and sprawling junipers, all of them grew out from this windswept coast.

Near the top of the hill a family of moose stood grazing. This small group had become well known to the locals who had named each one: the father, "Waldo," the mother, "Mildred," and their two kids, "Sally and Sarah."

As he neared the crescent overlooking the sea, the Labrador came into view, just before it veered north. From early childhood Philip knew this coast well with its deep coastal fiords and glacial carved valleys marking an otherwise unbroken coast all the way northward to the mysterious Torngat Mountains. From where Philip now stood, Belle Isle lay a good ways out and over the water to the east.

"All this is home." He spoke it then overlooking the Strait of Belle Isle and now deep in thought and remembering, he spoke it again.

Three Canada Geese with their nine goslings swam slowly by grazing off the shoreline, oblivious to the sun rising up through the morning mist, moving like a low-lying fog, changed forever by the light rays moving upwards from behind the island.

Gradually, the distant island rose as if from out of the water revealing as it did two loons, then those ever present seagulls swimming leisurely, all of them bobbing about in the gentle rhythm of the water. The book that he had put aside so often, slipped from his lap.

She came from behind him, framed by the hospital that loomed upwards, the newest part of which closed off the landscape from across the far end of the park. Philip's eyes listened to her soft gestures that told a story of the night before, a much different story than his. During the night when he had slept so soundly she sat beside her husband, tense, and listening to his every breath. Laura made her way to his bench and sat down very still, her hands lying limp on her lap.

For a long while neither spoke. Growing a bit uneasy, Philip strained forward to pick up the book and slowly stuffed it back into his satchel.

"Don't go, please," she whispered, and looked down, and then slowly she raised her head.

Somewhat startled, Philip turned sideways to face her and softly nodded. "I won't."

Some minutes before, they were total strangers, yet now he felt a growing bond through the space between them. In the stillness of that moment, Philip could feel her breath from across the bench and saw for the first time her pain.

Slowly, softly, faltering, Laura began to speak. "I came here... didn't want to go home just now... I called Susan after the ambulance left... She's flying in from St. John's later this morning... couldn't get an earlier flight, even then she had to drive a ways up the coast... she lives in the north part... it all came on so quickly...

"A few days before Richard slipped away, he whispered to me about how grateful he was that we had taken that trip to Norway last summer." Her gaze followed a pair of loons; suddenly one dove, and then the other, swooping under the surface of the river.

"Susan lives there now, Labrador, I mean. Susan writes how much she loves the people, the clean air, the sea, the simple quiet life, everything about it. She just becomes so restless here."

At first it seemed to take a strong effort to speak, yet as her words grew more urgent they now mingled with her native French. Laura told Philip that the family moved here from Alsace-Lorraine only three weeks after Susan was born.

"While still in France I lost two children before Susan – late miscarriages." Laura paused. "In my rage I vowed with Richard never ever to speak of this. Susan would never know."

Philip sat quietly.

Laura began to cry, at first softly. Soon her body convulsed into deep, rending sobs.

"I'm so sorry." Tentatively he reached for her hand that had now fallen down onto the bench between them. Rather than taking alarm as he feared, Laura softly squeezed his hand. She held it cold and unmoving.

"I knew this night would be his last," she whispered.

As the hours ebbed by slowly, inexorably, Laura sat alone for most of the night except for the nurse who came in every hour. "She brought in some tea once. Her name was Kara... and the young doctor, she was very kind and spoke to me several times about what to expect... and it did all happen, all through the night, the way she had said..."

Isabelle was her name, and she too was up all night meeting every stretcher the ambulance brought in to her. She met it all, the grief, the fear, the blood, the cursing, the anger, the death, yes, and the waste – and now, this morning, those hours had stripped her bare.

Every morning Isabelle walked home along the path by the river. She came by the bench where they were sitting and sat down beside Laura and slowly took her other hand, "I'm so sorry."

It was Laura who took Isabelle into her arms and held her. The soft wind blew and the morning rays shone into her long auburn hair still moist from the shower she had taken barely an hour before.

Isabelle left a few minutes later. Philip and Laura were again alone on the bench.

"We both thought there would be a little more time," Laura began, "but his head, his neck and back became unbearable last evening, and then by nightfall his stomach swelled so much. I thought it may have been his congestive heart again. Of course it wasn't."

Laura continued, faltering, crying softly.

"His skin and the whites of his eyes had turned a sick colour a week or so ago, and yesterday the vomiting... a lot of bleeding... Richard felt so tired all this week, and yesterday he just slept more. He looked spent.

"It was so quiet in the house all week, the stillness... I could hear it, feel it empty... I sat beside him much of the day, and I prayed. I was so scared..."

She and Richard loved one another and each had known that. In this final week, their eyes spoke wordlessly to one another of an intimacy nurtured through many years of joys and heartaches, and the unresolved tensions that lay locked under the surface unspoken, yet always painful.

Her grieving began some weeks after Richard was given the definitive diagnosis that yes, it is cancer. For Laura, the sense of inevitability became reality. Richard was going to die.

Long before that afternoon and night of waiting and listening she suffered the crushing ache that threatened to burst her chest, and dried up her mouth. Yet she had said nothing to Richard.

Laura ate little. Some days she cried for hours and seldom went to bed. Never had Laura faced death in anyone since the miscarriages. Last night, and several hours before the end, Richard requested Laura pray with him. Both of them, alone in the room – the last words Richard whispered were a paraphrase of Psalm 23: "I will not fear, for You, O Lord, are with me..."

As the hours passed, Laura felt Richard leaving her, withdrawing from her. With immense effort he slowly turned to the wall away from her. He no longer spoke.

As Laura sat beside her husband through the hours of this final night, she knew deep within herself that by the early dawn all would be very different. She would be walking home alone.

Out of their window that faced east, she watched the sunrise through the low, rolling mist over the water. Richard's breathing had become increasingly shallow in these final hours.

As she gazed out across the river, Richard became very still. Laura heard, turned slowly and knew that he was gone.

~~

Before Laura left Philip that morning several weeks ago, she spoke about Susan who, following her graduation as a nurse, settled in the east and far to the north, on the coast of Labrador among the Inuit. Last winter, Susan had written a letter as part of her diary wherein she described this land and people that seemed so much a part of her.

"I only read it last month," Laura whispered. "Here, I have kept part of it folded in my handbag."

Dear Mother and Dad:

…Some eight thousand years previous the Inuit had come here to hunt and to fish, to settle and raise families. They had abandoned their nomadic lifestyle, and came to the land reverently, and came to know it intimately, and the land and the sea in turn yielded up a faithful harvest. Thousands upon thousands of caribou passed by and through their villages as one herd; the hooded seal bred and whelped on the ice-floes off from shore; and the sea overflowed in ever-abundant fish.

Icebergs, sculptured as by a master artisan, calved off the shores of Ilulissat in Greenland, rising out of the water as sovereigns. Catching the cold ocean currents heading 'down' north and across to Baffin Island, they pass into the Labrador Sea, and are eventually seen from the shores off Nain and Cape Onion. Every one of these giants flow by in imperceptible slowness and majesty on their journey south along the shores of Newfoundland – and a few beyond...

I arrived at this northern fishing community two years ago under contract with the Labrador Health Services, founded at the turn of the last century and operated until recently by the Grenfell Mission. Sometimes we still call it that.

From the very moment I stepped off the turbo-beaver that flew me in from St. Anthony, I fell in love with these spontaneous people. An Inuit brass band met me, and a group of ladies from the Moravian Church singing hymns helped carry my suitcase and trunk to the clinic, which will be my home for the next five years...

Love, Susan

~ ~

The chimes from the bell tower struck on the hour that Susan's plane was expected to touch down. Deeply moved and too distracted to read, Philip watched as people gathered in the park. Most came in couples, some alone; there were those who carried books or kicked their soccer balls along, others brought only their lunch. A family sat together as if waiting for someone.

He first saw her as she strode through a cedar grove, a student in her early twenties, dressed only in a blue and white bikini, a carrying-bag and towel she carried slung over her left shoulder. From the water's edge she waded a few steps from shore, then dove gracefully, and for a while remained out of sight, emerging some meters further out. She continued in the direction of the island – the perfect rhythm of her breaststroke made it all appear as if in slow motion. Diving again beneath the waves she turned back to shore cutting through the water in a measured, masterful crawl.

She came to the shoreline and stepped out of the water, her skin glistening moist against the sun. She walked past Philip and smiled.

Close to where she had laid her towel and blanket, an older man sat, his Tilley hat slanted so as to shield his eyes from the advanced sun, now made all the brighter reflected by the water. He was also watching her.

She seemed to notice neither his presence, nor his gaze. As she lay down about a stone's throw away from him, a seagull landed and sauntered near anticipating some scrap of food.

At first Philip felt a pang of irritation at the man's attention – what right did he have to watch so intrusively?

It was then, Philip recognized him.

"His name is Arnold," he whispered to himself. Philip recognized his portrait on campus.

Years ago, Arnold, his wife and daughter, Amanda, had lived up the street. He was a quiet man, an academic. His wife, Tanya, was well spoken, an outgoing, fun-loving person. Nevertheless, she became, quite obvious to most everyone who knew the family, wearied with it all, yet "put up with it," as they say, to maintain the family's social connections.

Amanda was the only soul he had ever truly loved, and when Tanya left him for a much younger ski instructor, Arnold crashed.

Looking back, he could understand her estrangement, actually saw it as his fault. If the truth were known, he thought, it was he who had years before abandoned her. Arnold seemed never able to love his wife as either of them desired.

His teaching at the university filled up most of his life, and Tanya came to despise it all. Nevertheless, over the years, they were both silent about it, and the family pain became intractable. At night, both lay awake, alone in the darkness. They no longer touched. For Tanya, even the very thought of their former intimacy had become repulsive. Arnold knew it. Bedtime became unspoken intimidation.

Even before Tanya left with Amanda, Arnold began to drink excessively to block out the gnawing distance wedged between them.

Arnold came home from class one blustery afternoon in winter. The house had been cleaned. It was spotless. All his clothes had been washed and ironed. No one came home that night, and over the next days and months the house felt emptier to him than it would to the stranger who came in a year later to buy up the abandoned property - and Arnold never again saw his child, until several weeks ago.

Here near the banks of the river he now came to watch her. Amanda did not know him. She had been told, from the age of seven, that he never loved her – that is why they had left.

Amanda, however, remembered differently. She had eagerly anticipated bedtimes. Her father, a botanist, spent most of his time in the laboratory, or in the Arctic. When he returned home, Amanda treasured every moment of his presence – he treated her as if there was no one else. She read to him. They went through *Winnie the Pooh* so often, Amanda knew large parts of it by memory.

She loved it when he read Chaucer to her. At the beginning she understood very little of the "Olde English," as he called it, but the music and rhythm of the language, the way he read – that is what Amanda remembered.

Their walks through the conservation area impressed her deeply – he loved to teach, and she loved to listen. Even from so early an age, Amanda marveled at the beauty and complexities in creation.

She also remembered her father's love.

This is one reason she so loved being here by the water, looking over to the island, the sunrise, and the peace… the passing of a mallard duck with all her offspring filled Amanda with unspoken joy.

She was now in her first year of graduate studies and had returned to the city that was once her home.

In spite of what was said to her, Amanda missed her father and desired to know him, to be close to him. A month before, she had wandered into the biology department to see if anyone still knew him. She saw his portrait and stood in front of it for what seemed hours.

Ever since they had left home years before, her mother would not tolerate any mention of Arnold, nor of their previous life. She had attempted to convince Amanda that it was Roger who now loved her as his own, and their new life left no room for "hurtful memories." Nevertheless, it was Roger who often filled her with anxieties she had never before experienced.

For the first few years her mother seemed so happy that Amanda never dared to share these feelings with anyone. The time Amanda reached puberty was the first time she understood. From that time on her uneasiness rarely left – Amanda also knew that she would never trust him.

~ ~

From lying on her beach towel Amanda rose to spread lotion over her legs and arms. The breeze off the water felt cool against her skin. A copy of the Psalms fell out of her carrying bag. She loved these ancient poems her father had read to her, often using one of them for bedtime prayer: *I will lay me down in peace, and sleep: for thou, LORD, only makest me dwell in safety.*

With these memories of special times, Amanda felt a bond with her dad. This confirmed her through so many times when life shook to its foundation.

Nevertheless, this morning she had become very aware of the man's presence. A few days previous, Amanda came down with some friends to play volleyball. Arnold recognized her from a distance, and she saw him walking past. He stopped.

Amanda had felt his gaze long after, yet tried to ignore an excitement that came from seemingly nowhere. She was puzzled and did not quite understand this reaction to an older stranger. He continued on his walk.

Amanda lay back down but could not rest. The man sat watching.

Hesitant and very afraid, she got up and approached the picnic table.

Arnold saw her approach. He knew this moment would come. He had placed himself in just that proximity. Nevertheless, the brief time it took for Amanda to cross the distance between them became surreal. He had dreamt of this time, had anticipated it, yet a dread seized him so that he could not move. Those seconds as she walked over seemed an eternity. Amanda stood across from him. All of time seemed to refocus. They were both silent for what again seemed timeless.

"Dad?" She spoke it softly, hesitantly. Their eyes met, and held.

"Yes." He answered in a quivering near-whisper and felt the tears, but was afraid that they would destroy this moment he knew to be so fragile.

Amanda sat down across from him. "I thought that I had lost you," she said, again very quietly, and slowly she reached across the table, her soft hand now covering his.

~ ~

Philip also watched as two children kicked around a soccer ball. They seemed to belong to a family now gathering at another table. Their father came a bit later.

All morning he had sat with his younger son. Philip overheard some of the ensuing discussion – "It was confirmed only this morning, he is very sick," said his dad, "Leukemia… they may have caught it early…"

A few began to open their sandwiches. No one spoke. The children continued playing at some distance from the others.

A young woman dressed in a black pantsuit and tie crossed over the park lawn from the street. The two children ran up to her. She too was speaking on a cell phone and seemed to consider this a working lunch. She ignored the boys. The children's father approached her. They both spoke for a few minutes. He took her into his arms. She stiffened, and abruptly stepped back.

She appeared very angry and walked to the table, reached for a sandwich someone offered her and redialed the phone. She spoke deliberately, and seemed no longer to notice her estranged husband. He was now crying.

The older boy picked his mother some wild flowers that were growing in abundance along the shore. She took the flowers, still speaking on the phone, something about being late this afternoon.

Several minutes later, the flowers lay on the seat of a nearby bench, forgotten. She had left the family and walked up the hill to the hospital, the cell phone closely pressed to her ear.

Now some distance from the family, she demanded, loudly, to speak to her son's physician, immediately. Cynthia walked further on down the bicycle trail running alongside the river and away from the hospital. Her call was placed on hold, and she waited. He did not answer his page. Her son's pediatrician was with a patient and therefore, said the unknown lady on switchboard, provisionally unavailable.

In mounting frustration she screamed something about "your brazen insolence… if my baby dies…" She began to tremble and the cell phone fell from her grasp, and bounced under a deep purple lilac bush next to the pathway. Staggering to a park bench, she sat down, and stared vacantly ahead of her.

~ ~

A year after Cynthia married she was offered a position with a prestigious law firm in town, working as a criminal trial lawyer. During these past six years she built up a very competent practice dealing primarily in women's issues. When arguing a lucrative divorce case, "she will fight for every gold filling," her friends said of her.

Last week Cynthia was able to work from her condominium while she kept her son home from school. The child's name was Llewellan, their third son. He became very sick by his second day with her. By week's end he was in a lot of pain, and crying through most of the night.

Cynthia refused to allow any physician to examine him and purchased instead alternative remedies across the counter. In a defiant and illogical sort of way, she knew these would definitely "work." After all, she trusted no one to inform her otherwise. By Sunday, Llewellan might be able, she hoped, to return to his father and brothers.

Cynthia had taken the initiative and divorced Ron just last year. For some years he had taught history and mathematics in a senior second-ary school, but lately decided his first love had always been, and still was, working with wood.

"Love the smell of it," he once flippantly confessed at a staff dinner.

"You insipid fool," came Cynthia's swift and bitter response.

So, every weekday morning, while she headed for the office on Oxford Street, Ron walked out to the garage he had recently converted into his woodworking shed, and that is where he spent most days. The boys always knew their dad to be "out back" when they ran in from school.

While pregnant with their third child, Cynthia stayed home. To avoid pre-term labour she was prescribed bed rest during the final four weeks. It had been a difficult pregnancy. Her blood pressure remained elevated and labile throughout. She had never before felt so exhausted. Neither had she ever been so depressed.

Following the birth of Llewellan, Cynthia was unable to feed him. Neither was she able, for a long while, to care for him in any way.

Weeks later, Cynthia began to seethe with anger. Occasionally she punched and pinched her husband time after time. By her disturbed mood swings she controlled everyone in the family. The boys were almost always on the verge of tears. The oldest, Tommy, complained of constant stomach pains, and stopped eating. Matthew lived with an all-consuming anxiety for fear lest one of his parents leave. His marks in school dropped. As the school semester passed, he thought that underachieving might distract his parents from one another's jarring conflicts and bring them together over one concern, himself.

Cynthia prided herself in her denial of God – and following her post-partum depression, "death" was a word never permitted in her presence by anyone. If someone dared, she reacted as if in morbid fear.

Ron never understood this, and she never spoke of it.

He did know her father. "Sir," as everyone addressed him, had been in World War II, an infantry leader at the front. One sultry afternoon in France, he led his men against a German unit. He suspected enemy combatants were entrenched in a small, by now, deserted town.

This became a lamentable misjudgment. Without further confirmation, his men opened fire and grenades were thrown. In the end the bodies of the townsfolk – men, women, and children – lay dead or seriously wounded. One small boy had died in the arms of his grandmother. She too lay dead, riddled with bullets.

A sniper shot from the edge of the forest. His best friend died in his arms. He tried in vain to place pressure over a gaping abdominal wound. The priest from the only church in town also lay dead – he had tried desperately to warn the Allies of the families still left and ran into a barrage of her father's bullets.

Most of the enemy had retreated to the woods further north, presumably so as not to jeopardize the families in the inevitable crossfire!

"Sir" could never forgive himself for that repugnant blunder, the foremost of which was to live and not to have died. He came home from the front scarred and frightened, a man who lived with his family as an isolated father and husband. He rarely slept and lived his years in fret and conscience, shut off as if in a room by himself.

"Sir" became obsessed with his story and seemed compelled to tell everyone anywhere, over and over again. He often wept openly during the telling. Cynthia bore the brunt of it all.

She never knew a time when her mother, Bette, ever came in to defend her. In time Bette had dissociated herself from the recurrent horror of her husband's compulsive retelling, and her daughter's pain.

Throughout her childhood and adolescence, Cynthia became haunted nightly by the scene in that French village repeatedly and vividly described to her.

Cynthia sat on the park bench for what to her seemed hours. It was very quiet. Rather than having walked in the direction of the hospital, Cynthia found herself as before, near the shores of the river, though further east, and very much alone.

As she sat looking across to the island, Cynthia remembered her summers, now long past, spent on the northernmost tip of Newfoundland. Her aunt lived in a town, Raleigh, a quiet fishing community on the north Atlantic, near the exposed Limestone Barrens of Burnt Cape.

Cynthia loved the tiny and rare plant life thriving there between the rocks, like the Roundleaf Orchids, the Netveined Willow and the River Beauty, all hugging the ground, sheltering themselves against the cold North Atlantic winds.

The juniper trees, some many hundreds of years old, have grown only inches from the ground. She became awestruck by the ancient fossils that date back millions of years when the fresh water sea had once covered the area. Here she came to appreciate the magnificent windswept landforms, and the mysterious sea cave, called by the locals Big Oven, and, Oh yes, the peace, the repose away from the oppressive life back home.

Cynthia would forever and clearly remember those nights when she herself had gone to bed, listening as her aunt knelt alongside the bed praying for her. Aunt Rita would do this faithfully every night of every year she was able.

She died several summers back. When the letter came, Cynthia was in the middle of a lucrative case. She paused for a few moments before slipping the letter under a pile of unanswered correspondence.

Berries, Tickles and Saltwater Ice

This afternoon Cynthia missed her deeply. Aunt Rita, solid as the rocks of Burnt Cave and loving to her as no other. She felt the loss and the remembering like a hole in her soul. Cynthia became breathless. The long suppressed ache pounded like a relentless wave upon wave. She curled up on the bench, overlooking the river stretching east, groaned, and sobbed her unspoken grief.

Ron was sitting beside Llewellan. The child had slept most of today. It was midnight.

She walked in slowly, quietly, noticed first only by her mother-in-law who sat knitting in the far corner. She smiled at Cynthia and did not seem to remember her cold, even hostile attitude earlier in the day.

Cynthia came in and stood beside the child's father, no longer her husband – it all seemed suddenly bizarre. Llewellan was their son. Why is it all so different now?

She had the urge to lay her hand on Ron's shoulder, but did not.

She offered to sit up the night while he and his mother went home to sleep. He wondered rather if she would like a coffee and croissant. He knew, they both knew of course, of an all-night café around the corner.

As the hours wore on, she told him about the afternoon, how she remembered, and how she cried into the evening at the very same time her son lay in the hospital so sick, and how she had suddenly felt so appallingly self-centered and judged… but that she also felt clean and unashamed for the first time in years.

"It was nothing in myself," she said. She told him all about her aunt praying.

"I always felt so stained… yet my times with her in that northern village, in those brief summers, I felt so safe, so pure there on the cove. Auntie kept saying two things I will remember always, that " 'tis God Who has given us everyt'ing we could ne'er deserve…" and one time later, "You need to keep yer roots, me darlin', here on the land by dis 'ere sea. You come back 'ere someday… den you'll understand… when the time's ready for you…

"I am so sorry, Ron… please let me sit the night with Llewellan, and tomorrow…"

~ ~

Over the next days and nights, rain and wind pounded the shore. Thunder peeled deeply across the river like kettledrums through all the corners of a concert hall. Lightning lit up the sky behind the islands with awesome fingers of power.

Philip thought about the families, about the boy desperately sick, and about the child's family stretched and wrenched at a time when he needed them all together.

There were Arnold and Amanda after years of separation. He wondered what had happened between them these past days after they slowly left the table hand in hand that morning of discovery, hopeful of newness and healing.

This also may be the day of the funeral for Laura's husband. Philip really missed her after she left, and still, even today. There was something in her visit, something hidden and mysterious that gripped him.

… and then, there were all those other people who had come out that morning, all carrying their own stories, most of them playing, some talking about term papers and exams. To many of them, the world of the others around them, the Lauras and the Arnolds, might well be deemed intrusive and inconsequential.

In these last few stormy days Philip did read and indeed finished the book he carried to the river that morning. Tonight there was a Bach concert at the university, the timeless B-minor Mass, Bach's "dance before God," a work Philip had, for all the years he could remember, deeply loved as no other.

By evening the rain had somewhat abated. He was quite prepared to attend and know no one, except his niece Evelyn who sang in the choir, and for that reason alone he would have gladly come.

Taking his place in the front row of the mezzanine, Philip began reading the program while Amanda and her father took their seats across from him to the side. Philip glanced up. Once again, as in that morning, days before, she recognized him and smiled.

Tonight she looked so poised and beautiful.

Several weeks following the Bach concert, Philip and Amanda stood on the shores of the river. As sunset descended, lights from the island began flickering over the darkening water. Several dozen sailboats tacked reluctantly towards the marina. A foghorn from a distant lighthouse, a long summoning cry from a pair of loons, and the shallow waves breaking on shore beneath their feet were all that broke the stillness that engulfed them.

They sat on a bench. She touched his hand and leaned against him. He moved his arm around her shoulder and Amanda snuggled in closer. They sat there quietly...

Much later, she revealed to Philip that there had been years of the locust that sought to derail and ravish her time and again — yet could not. Time and again, Roger tried to sabotage her schooling, her relationships — he had become morbidly possessive and jealous. He flew into a rage before her high school prom and refused to allow her boyfriend into the house. After she did leave, Roger also left and waited for them outside the school. What was intended to be an evening of carefree fun, became a never-to-be-forgotten night in hell.

"It was the day of my seventeenth birthday late in spring. Tanya came into my bedroom, 'I just heard, your dad has died,' she stated triumphantly, 'an alcohol overdose... wouldn't you just know it,' and walked out. The right side of my body felt suddenly numb. I stumbled into the bathroom...

"During my first semester at university, Roger often prowled around campus stalking me, but kept his distance. I became distracted and depressed. Tanya denied everything. At the same time she blamed me for 'arousing your father'.

"Tanya came to my residence one night shortly after, cursed me, and screamed at me for betraying the family.

"Confused and crushed into little pieces, I sat and rocked and rocked all night. I thought of nothing. That night I felt nothing but a consuming sadness and headache."

Amanda would have been alone for her first Christmas at university had it not been for the Newfoundland pastor and his family. "They opened their home for me and some friends. We stayed on campus during Christmas.

"Following the midnight Service at the church, all ten of us sat around the fireplace laughing and chatting while enjoying a hot drink mixed from

Newfoundland bakeapple. At noon, Christmas day, the family opened their kitchen for us. Rosemary, the pastor's wife, prepared the turkey, the dressing and all that made Christmas dinners so special.

"This home and these friends became new family for the next four years, years that became for me times of salvation and thanksgiving."

~ ~

Susan gave up her vacation to follow the Inuit to their fishing and hunting camps north of Hebron, past the now long abandoned Moravian mission, and to the edge of the Torngat Mountain range. She learned to catch Arctic Char, to skin caribou, and to drink from cold glacial streams. It was here on this land they knew as no other, that the Inuit felt free. Being a family-oriented culture, they accepted Susan, the nurse, as one of their own.

It was here, camped on the shores of the Labrador Sea, that Susan received the relayed phone message from Laura that her father was in intensive care. Susan assured her mother that she would try to come quickly. A plane at the RCMP post up the coast, about two hours flying time, would come first thing in the morning.

Fire crackled through the palpable silence of the Labrador night. Many Inuit at the camp came and sat with her, a comforting presence with not a word ever spoken. Aurora borealis exploded and pulsated expansively across the northern skies. Green, violet and red patches dancing, twisting and arcing.

In the south, words like awesome have become meaningless and flippant, not here. Here amongst creation's breathtaking, even numinous grandeur, Susan pondered – there is no word. Her Inuit friends knew it simply as a mystery, and desired to know it in no other way.

~ ~

Susan arrived several days late. Laura had initially met the scheduled flight unaware of the impending circumstances that delayed Susan's arrival. The chilling winds in that early morning suddenly gusted and the sea pounded relentlessly against the shore. All that day and the next, no plane could land anywhere around St. Anthony and along the coast north, past the Torngats and into Ungava Bay.

Susan had always felt safe and insulated in this land, and it was usually here in its awesome quiet that she became best able to sort through her feelings. This unpredicted storm afforded her the space she needed to be alone before returning for the funeral.

Laura could not understand her daughter's seemingly passionate love for the far north, repeatedly consoling herself that it is just another passing phase of a restless girl.

Susan's lateness was thought very inconsiderate, and she deserved much more from Susan, her only child. Laura responded to her own discouragement with angry outbursts.

Nevertheless, Susan was coming home and would naturally pass off her phase, Laura presumed: "Such a life that she was now living could not continue."

"What would happen now… about Susan… you know, her leaving again…?" Laura's friends inquired.

"She has too much rock-bottom sense and is far too level-headed," Laura confidently answered, "She's home now."

Susan's parents lived their lives in familiar surroundings. They had a few friends with whom they often vacationed on luxury cruises or rented a beach-side condominium in the Cayman Islands. As a child Susan often did not know where.

Early on, years ago, Susan began turning away from her parent's expectations for her. Laura wished for Susan to become a teacher. Rather, she earned an honours science degree in nursing.

Months before graduation she had applied to the Grenfell Mission for a five year northern nursing position on the Labrador. Susan was accepted. Her parents became dismayed and angry. They had come to expect the predictable and the settled for their own lives. This extended to their daughter. To them Susan had become headstrong, heartless and unruly.

Laura censured her choice. Their friends agreed. Her father said nothing.

Susan had been very close to her father, a relationship at times resented by Laura. He understood her longing for a change, her desire since childhood to learn about distant peoples. Her program at university had offered her options, special interest courses, and she worked them in, all she could handle – indigenous cultures of the north, earth sciences and geology in particular.

Laura considered these courses "too masculine" and her years at school "now wasted." They considered the "Eskimo" barbarians and the land in the far north "inhospitable, most definitely crude."

On Susan's last night before leaving for St. Anthony, Laura burst out,

"I am – no we both are – very disappointed in you – no angry – that you are defying us. Tell us, what have your father and I done to you that you have now turned your back on us, on our hopes for you all these years? This is nothing but..." Laura's voice trailed off into an inaudible whisper.

These words cut deeply, spoken on their last evening meal together before Susan.

Susan left the dining room quietly, alone. She felt cut off. Laura and Richard did not see their daughter to the airport in the morning.

These tensions again erupted during Susan's stay for the funeral. Laura encouraged her to stay "home," but Susan no longer could. She knew her home, and it was a thousand miles northeast, among a people Laura in mounting frustration and anger labeled "savages."

Laura felt Susan abruptly pull away from her, and became aware that she had crossed a line from which she could never retreat.

Quite possibly advanced by her own grief, Laura could not see Susan's mature serenity and poise. During her two years in the north, Susan became known for her decisive interventions in crises, and her total lack of any pretensions. The Inuit of Nain trusted her implicitly.

Relatives flew in from distant places, and friends dropped in to express condolences and bring freshly baked pastries. Yet it was in the evening, even more so following the funeral, that Susan and her mother were left by themselves.

Laura's expectations were, as she often explained to her friends, that Susan would move back, at least into the area "now that you have got this adventure out of your system," she had repeated to Susan one evening rather curtly.

Berries, Tickles and Saltwater Ice

"My home, Mother, is now in the north and I shall be leaving on Saturday. The nursing office in St. Anthony has granted me leave until Monday."

A tense silence ensued. Laura fidgeted uncomfortably. "Is that all the time you requested?"

"Yes... I'd like to tell you more about my work there, and the people. Newfoundland is such a beautiful land, a quiet land, Mother, and the sea and the rocks and mountains in the far north, the northern lights with their colourful streaks and pillars floating and dancing across the skies. You can never hear, or feel such quietness. I even heard my own jugular vein pulsate standing as we did on the rocky shores of Nachvak Fjord in the Torngat Mountains. One weekend we flew in and camped, caught a few Arctic Char and..."

"Who is *we*," Laura broke in, sharply.

"Martin and I. He flew me north to see 'the most beautiful spot on earth.' He assured me of that..."

"And was it?"

"Yes."

The grandfather clock chimed ten. In the tense silences between mother and daughter, it seemed to echo sharply against the bare hardwood floors. Neither spoke until Laura posed the question she herself dreaded to ask.

"Do you love him?"

"Yes, I do."

"What does he do there?"

"He's a pilot for the Grenfell hospital, transporting patients to the hospital and back home again. Martin brought... flew me down south to catch my plane last Sunday. He had always wanted to be a pilot and he is such a good one. He asked if I would bring him back a collection of poems by E.J.Pratt. Martin graduated from Memorial University in earth sciences... Oh yes, he will meet me in Gander this coming Sunday morning."

"Where is Martin from?"

"He is Inuit, Mother, born in northern Greenland, just across from Ellesmere Island, north of Baffin Island and across the strait. Coming from Greenland, Martin and his family are Lutheran, and devoted Christians..." Susan paused, "and so am I."

Laura suddenly apprehensive, her voice quivering: "What is an Inuit... an Eskimo?"

"Yes. They are wonderful people, Mother, who believe that God created everything and everyone in a sacred balance, that we are all bonded together, the land, the sea, the animals. This is so evident in Martin and his family. His father is a professional carver who has moved to Baker Lake, that's in Nunavut. Martin's parents are both at camp where I am stationed for a while. It's an Inuit hunting and fishing area at the foot of those Torngat Mountains..."

Laura was no longer listening. She rose and walked silently up the stairs. Susan heard the bedroom door close quietly.

Laura remained in her bedroom through the following morning. By noon she came down and met Susan in the kitchen saying that she had dinner to prepare for some friends.

"Their boy, Llewellan, has leukemia. His doctor readmitted him into the pediatric oncology ward last weekend."

"His parents are divorced, aren't they?"

"Yes, and it appears that they've come together over this. The boy's father, Ron, sits with him most of the day. Cynthia, she's a lawyer, comes in after work. I saw them walking along the river together just yesterday holding hands."

As Susan flew along the coast from St. Anthony, north to the camp she had left the week before, she watched the icebergs below her floating south along "The Alley." In the end, her mother still could not understand how Susan was "willing to throw away everything that we have ever given you..."

Martin saw Susan staring down into the passing land below them, and the tears she had not wanted him to see.

An hour into the trip, he reached across and lightly touched her hand. She held his and began to talk about her dad, and her grief, and her mother who has always resisted the paths Susan chose. And now this...

"We had a terrible scene before I left. She wanted me to stay home, settle down and be responsible… and I told her, 'I am.'" Laura had the final word.

She sat beside him for a long time. Neither spoke. Susan looked into his face. "I am home," she said disarmingly.

The plane flew deeper north and for a brief diversion Martin circled a caribou herd. Out on the ice floe, a polar bear with her two cubs looked up before she dove below the ice in search of food.

II

Nachvak Fjord, North Labrador

Four months later, Isabelle applied to stand in for another physician at the Grenfell Mission. Like several others at the hospital, she had moved in from Kingston, a university town on the mainland to a coastal peoples with deep, established roots and very close kinship ties. Their personal warmth was genuine and unencumbered. Their love for the sea infuses the very core of their lives, and only in the lifetime of a scattered few will this ever be effaced.

For centuries these men have risked their lives daily. Their women stand by them bravely. In the earliest dawn of every morning, the men leave and the women never really know if they will return. The soup on the kitchen stove will be steaming hot when they do. Oftentimes they do not.

These fisher folk had settled in St. Anthony, many of them drawn by steady employment at the hospital founded at the turn of the last century by a missionary doctor.

Years before, Isabelle had read about Dr. Wilfred Grenfell who came to the coast. He was appalled at the prevalence of tuberculosis and the high death rate amongst the fishing families throughout the outports and coves stretching north as far as Hebron on the Labrador. Later he stood firm against the greedy merchants and powerful bureaucrats in St. John's. Many of them lived to bulge their own purse and lust for power. As a consequence they held the coastal people hostage to their abject poverty.

This earnest and gifted physician set up a mission to the North Sea fishermen that today has become more complex and far-reaching than he ever envisioned.

Isabelle was often called on to escort seriously ill patients from the nursing stations on the Northern Peninsula and Labrador to the hospital in St. Anthony. Her first call came from Nain.

Susan Thomas, the station nurse, diagnosed a heart attack in a lady who had been unable to get out of bed this morning. She had severe chest and upper back pain the day before and by this morning her angina had become very unstable.

Additionally, in years past, she has had three consecutive miscarriages. Her son came for Susan before breakfast. Susan called St. Anthony for a medivac.

The physician in the plane and Susan had been on the wireless over the past few hours. Both women were aware of the patient's fragility, and of the intensifying storm moving in, currently pounding North-West River to the south.

The plane circled Nain in a rapid descent. Landing on the frozen bay, it taxied over the frozen snow as close to shore as possible. Isabelle disembarked and followed Susan walking briskly up an incline that led to the family's home.

Once there, she realized quickly that the lady would not survive an evasive and circumvented flight to St. Anthony. Oxygen and an intravenous were already in place. Susan had dealt with the immediate crisis, and thankfully Isabelle's medic's bag contained most of what else was needed.

A group of men carried her stretcher over to the nursing station where Isabelle contacted the cardiologist in St. Anthony. The connection arrived faint and static, then died out altogether. The blizzard suddenly hit Nain in full fury.

Isabelle and Susan watched over their patient all that morning and through the day. Her pain abated. The storm rendered visibility nil.

At mealtime that first day Susan disclosed that she had been raised in Kingston.

"After graduation just two years ago and some months, I applied to work here on the Labrador."

"Your last name has a familiar ring. Did your father pass away at the hospital about six months ago?"

"Yes, he did."

"Your mother's name, can it be Laura? If so, I'm the doctor who attended your Dad the night he died."

Working side by side these days marked the beginning of their enduring bond and friendship.

Two days later the storm's grip weakened sufficiently for Isabelle and her patient to fly on to the Curtis Hospital in St. Anthony.

~ ~

Isabelle completed her six month locum in St. Anthony. Nevertheless, from the hour her plane left the coast, Isabelle knew in her heart what she really desired. The life Isabelle led in the city and the life she had lived in northern Newfoundland were just far too different. Furthermore, she had fallen in love with the unfathomable sea in all her diversity of life, on her surface and in her depths.

The sea floor, as it moves from here and into the Arctic, is home to innumerable marine invertebrates, living in brilliant and variegated communities hitherto unknown. Isabelle became awestruck as she read about the whales, and the known fact that they can hear one another over the distance of untold miles.

She wanted to appreciate the mysteries of that life.

Isabelle had never given serious thought as to how eons upon eons of ice and water have sculpted such a beautiful coast that frames this island, or to an iceberg calved from the glaciers of Greenland's deep and mosaic icecap, joining from there colossal convoys moving across the Labrador Sea, and are eventually seen along the coast of Newfoundland.

She wanted to know more about the very ancient rock formations that had given the Island its name, the Rock, the pure air and spectacular sunsets, the people – and the peace.

She wrote her intentions to Susan.

~ ~

Martin Peter, the pilot, was born in Ilulissat, Greenland, the bays and coastline of the awesome Ilulissat Icefjord.

His parents migrated across Davis Strait and settled in remote Grise Fiord on Ellesmere Island when he was ten. His father, Johanssen, spent a great deal of time on the coast hunting seal, caribou and the occasional polar bear, while his mother Martinna sewed the clothes for the family from the skins her husband brought home from the hunt. Martin grew up intimately acquainted with the attitudes and traditions of his people.

One early April morning Martin flew into the fishing camp north of Hebron. He reported a small shoal of seal he had seen on a broken-off ice pan about a mile off shore.

Four men in camp immediately ran to their sealskin kayaks, rifles and harpoons in hand. Stealthily each came to the floe of ice and approached the several dozen adults within range.

A sudden staccato crack from the rifles momentarily broke the waiting silence.

Watching atop the cliff on shore, Susan watched with the others from camp as the men on the ice loaded the five carcasses and brought them to shore.

Later, everyone sat around the central fire, the talk irrepressibly light, and altogether shared in the feast of fresh berries, seal and arctic char. Every portion of each animal hunted that day and every other would be used and shared – not a sinew wasted. This is the ancient Inuit way.

An hour later Martin proceeded on south to North-West River. On his way the nurse from Hopedale had called requesting a medivac. A youngster had an inflamed and threatening appendix. This was Martin's first call to the area since the previous spring.

In late March, two men had started down the coast in skidoos. Both were native to the area and seasoned in the ways of the wind and ice movement off shore this time of year.

Carson made light of her concern and insisted that the ice across the bay held firm. His wife, Martha, had suggested they rather leave the shore with a dog team. In any event the the dogs would smell any water and unsafe ice, and so refuse to run. Carson made light of her caution and insisted that he knew his way over the bay.

Rather than following one another across the ice, for unknown reasons they rode abreast. As a consequence, Carson did not to see the spray being thrown out back by their machines until he slowed to check their bearing to the shore. It was then he realized, both were in very serious jeopardy. He did not know, however, how long their skidoos had kicked up the water. If they slowed too much, or stopped, the ice could not hold.

Carson tried to yell out. His friend could not hear him. The engines were too loud.

Terror gripped him, yet his friend remained oblivious. Carson attempted to overtake him and he did, motioning for his friend to immediately turn into shore full speed. His friend stopped the skidoo not understanding, or hearing.

The back end of his machine was the first to slide under the ice. With a massive effort, he tried to jump free, but could not. Carson turned around quickly and in full throttle screamed past his friend, grabbing an arm as he did. He had already been submerged up to the waist and more ice was caving in.

Carson could not stop. He had clutched his friend's arm with superhuman strength and continued to fly past the hole in the ice.

At first Carson did not know if his friend was really on board. He was. Carson continued to hang onto him and raced towards shore.

Two boys were playing on land next to the water and saw what was happening. They ran towards the nearest house for help. Carson got there ahead of them struggling to hold on to the now limp body of his friend.

He was conscious when they laid him on the kitchen floor, near the stove. One of the boys ran to the nursing station.

Carson's friend began to scream in pain. He was frozen from the waist down. The family brought a blanket. He continued to scream and cry and shake. "Jesus, Jesus…"

No one but a little girl saw him as he managed to pull himself over to a rifle leaning against the wall near by.

The nurse running toward the house heard the shot ring out from in the kitchen. When she ran in, his body lay slumped over a chair. Blood from his chest spattered against the wall.

Martin flew in two hours later. The RCMP released the body for transport to St. Anthony.

~ ~

Dear Mother:

When I came home for Dad's funeral you asked me about "resettlement fuss" in the north which the television news had "gone on about."

Some years ago now, many Inuit had attempted to re-settle in Nain from coastal communities further north. This resettlement program initiated by the government was based largely on deception and coercion. They called it a "disposition" of native peoples. Many claim that it was in fact racism.

The bureaucrats decided that it was too expensive to assist these coastal peoples with their education, medical, social and spiritual needs. Therefore they must be moved on. Without consultation, the Inuit of Hebron, were relocated in larger communities further south.

The Inuit were promised jobs, adequate housing, better food and education — in the process what they actually received with the loss of their land, were social breakdown, overcrowding, alcoholism, rape, and a terrifying threat to their proud and ancient identity. Recreation, and profit for the southern tourist industry, gross ignorance and greed from the government in the south came in to profane the land of their fathers. For a time, the Inuit stood by and grieved this most profound loss.

This cruel program was also decreed on the Island of Newfoundland – small communities, home to families for centuries, coerced to uproot under similar threats...

Years ago the area around Englee on the Northern Penninsula had undergone a near cataclysmic social upheaval. The 1950s and 60s were the years of forced resettlement into "growth centres." Most of the sea-shore cove people of Hooping Harbour on the northeast coast, led by their gritty pastor, defied the government's coercion. They did so by floating all their houses, stages, general stores, and church from home, north along the coast, down through the Bay, past Englee on its northern headland, and from there, on to its inland shore. Here the fishing families of Hooping Harbour established the successful community of Bide Arm. Their loss could have been overwhelming but today they live a full and vibrant life.

Another injustice, cruelty, if you wish, that coastal Newfoundlanders faced involved foreign over fishing. For years strangers from across the Atlantic, some from the U.S. and some even from home, came to the Island's waters. They scraped, raked and tore up the sea bottom. They pulled up anything and everything, respecting nothing and in the process destroying the habitat and breeding grounds for many species. The cod fish became seriously depleted, and now the possibility for recovery is seriously stressed. Rapacious greed, overzealous competition and plunder, the arrogant dismissal of the scientific evidence has eventuated in the rape of the sea, and in the end contributed significantly to re-settlement and depression.

This was not the fault of inshore fishermen, like our friend Wilf, geared largely to support their families and communities up and down the coast. Nevertheless, they bore the brunt of it all. The loss became incalculable.

Berries, Tickles and Saltwater Ice

The moratorium of 1992 announced the collapse of the cod fishery off the coast of Newfoundland and Labrador.

This government moratorium disposed a coastal culture. Again as in years gone by, and further north, the politicians in their willful ignorance displaced and resettled many families into growth communities with "better opportunities." If people resisted the government threatened to withdraw health and educational structures - much as with the Inuit further north. Another blow was their offer of some meagre outlay of money to assist in this transition. Nonetheless, a token "fix" cannot give people back their roots, identity and pride.

The day the announcement came, the men on the Cape gathered around an old black and white television set to listen, and the words that came through shattered Wilf's world: the moratorium was immediate - no more cod was to be fished, and even those caught in their nets that morning were to be thrown back. If only one single cod already netted was loaded into the boats, the politicians threatened a severe financial penalty.

The folks of Cape St. Charles had been warned of a disaster impending for most Newfoundlanders. Only a very few had anticipated the length and breadth of it. Everyone in the crowded house by the bay that morning stood around in stunned silence.

An elderly man, Greg Bartlett, walked out onto the bridge of the house, lit his pipe and looked across the bay. "What are we going to do?" he whispered, barely audible. Those were the only words he spoke all that day, and all the next week

For them this day marked their darkest hour.

Love, Susan

~ ~

As a young lad one early morning many years ago, his dad woke him. Rather than go schooling today, Wilf was told to come fishing.

"The rest can wait," his dad said in a determined voice.

For the now greater part of his life, Wilf rose early most every morning, ate a quick breakfast and walked out to the stage where his skiff lay moored. He and most other men from coastal communities no longer fished further out to sea. While fishing so far offshore many became vulnerable to illness and fatigue. Some, however, left the inshore and did go further and further out. Some of their boats were not constructed for the high seas. Many never returned.

It had been a good life. He and Marjorie lived most of their years in Cape Charles, and there raised six children, the youngest, Karen being seven, the eldest Gladina now eighteen. The family scrimped and saved for her to realize a dream she had held onto since childhood.

"She's now gone up to St. John's to learn nursing at Memorial," Wilf proudly announced to anyone who would listen.

The fishermen of Newfoundland's coast first noticed a problem back in the 1980s. Fewer and fewer fish were being netted, and for them and their families it had become increasingly difficult to make ends meet.

Wilf listened to the many reasons and rumours thrown out and about to explain this decline in fish. Nevertheless, he knew, and they all knew, the answer politicians avoided. Wilf and the others up and down the coast knew that for years the offshore fishery came to be dominated by large deep-sea vessels from Europe and elsewhere – even some from Newfoundland.

Wilf, his family and others moved from the rocky shores of Cape St. Charles on the south Labrador. The families had lived and fished there for generations. That is what they did, and far more fundamentally, that was who they were, outport fishermen.

Like many Newfoundlanders, Wilf knew the intrinsic bond he shared with the community, and to the land and sea, and to God – from experience they knew Him as their Rock, the net-mender of their lives and very often their shelter in time of storms, imagery that echoes a reality few others really understand.

Together with the Inuit further north, these stalwart and resilient people of the Island's coast could be manipulated and beat up, but never defeated. Still yet, a few were.

The Grenfell Hospital offered Wilf regular employment. However, there remains for him a private reality that only Marjorie knows, nevertheless shared by thousands - that is his intense longing to be out on the sea. Wilf knows it, he says, during the long waking hours of many nights as a "gut-wrenching and lonely hell."

Occasionally he is seen standing atop the cliffs on Fishing Point. There he stands motionless and silent for hours, his hands clenched, his face red with rage seeing the "city of lights," a long line of foreign trawlers dragging many miles out to sea.

Wilf and his family knew this would be far more painful for some. His own brother could never come to terms with it all, the resettling, the moratorium, and the loss of his home.

Last Spring the ice stayed. Breakup had not come and the ice remained unbroken for miles out to sea, some claimed two hundred. The sea groaned and heaved under the imprisoning and merciless ice. A few scattered areas eventually broke up, yet with the lack of drifting ice no one could fish – and the seal had not come in either. A week previous, a polar bear had ventured as far south as St. Anthony in a desperate search of food. She was spotted in town and chased back onto the ice lumbering ahead of a police cruiser.

The winter had been long and brutal. During the past several weeks Wilf's cousin, Cedar, stood on the shore for hours looking out to sea, although for him time no longer existed. One early morning the sky, the ice, the sun, he himself, all became one, like Vincent van Gogh's beautiful painting, Wheat Field with Crows. In a personal and expressive manner, Van Gogh paints vast expanses of wheat under a dark and stormy sky. The field, the sky and the crows show no interface, nor distinctive form. It's a very unsettled piece. Painted a short while before he died, it echoes a profound crisis, his own terrible loneliness and sadness.

Cedar often stood and stared at Wilf's print of the painting for hours.
Then one afternoon he began his lonely walk into the blurring oneness
ahead always receding, no longer seeing, surrounded by formlessness and
frozen silence…

~ ~

Philip had always loved the Island, and its astonishing beauty. The grandeur
of Gros Morne Park shaped by glaciers and a myriad of tectonic upheavals,
its hiking trails, its alpine plateau, its forests and clear water lakes, the coastal
lowlands, its fossils once part of an ancient sea life, its stillness and peace, all
made this region his favorite on earth south of the Torngats.

Merely the thought of walking on this granite-laid land formed a thousand eons ago makes him feel as he does when lying on his back somewhere
in this untaken wilderness looking out into the vastness of the universe, its
infinite hosts of stars and galaxies, million upon millions of them, and each
of the innumerable millions far more immense than his own.

Philip never tired of looking over the horizon where tan and greenish
colored surfaces of the tablelands called peridotite have been pushed up
from the earth's upper mantle myriads of years before. Because of this they
are alien rocks, toxic actually. Being loaded in magnesium nickel and iron,
these tablelands cannot sustain life. Their magnificence and mystery, and
the immense power that pervaded the earth in such creation would subdue
Philip to silence and profound awe.

Amanda expressed a desire to see this place, to feel the brisk sea spray
against her face, and to understand why Philip, her husband, loved this land
so very much.

They were married in the stone church on campus.

"This has been such an amazing year," Amanda thought as her father,
nearly unknown to his daughter a year ago, walked beside her down
the aisle.

In all this year she had not seen her mother, or Roger. Nevertheless, Amanda heard from others.

Roger and her mother had found out about the wedding. Tanya fumed with rage. Roger who worked as a "master trainer" at a fitness club took leave for a week, "to save my marriage," he claimed.

Inflamed, Roger began combing the university campus. He had no clear idea what to say had he and Amanda met – just anything to coerce her away from the marriage. He needed to tell her that she filled, no inspired every moment of every hour of his life. If she only knew how much he loved her, desired her, needed to possess her completely – no, Roger could not tell her that, he thought, not yet.

Roger spent days walking, sitting in shadows. He did not know her friends, not even the name of the man Amanda was engaged to marry.

Tanya wrote letters in search for her. She had to find her. Every night Roger came home, and their frenzy grew more intense. Tanya became enmeshed in his desperation and jealousy; she felt his lust – yes, how can Amanda do this to them!

Perhaps if she spoke with the priest of the campus church, he would understand what this would do to the family. Tanya drove the six hours into town.

The priest stood firm and would say nothing. She yelled curses and became irrational. He summoned the police who held her overnight.

Roger and Tanya did, somehow, learn the time and day of the wedding. They would both be there, together, though in her nervous haste Tanya misread the date and wrote it down for a week later. Arnold discreetly hired two men to stand as guards outside the church during the wedding and outside the Queen's Faculty Club during the time of the banquet.

~ ~

Philip and Amanda drove into Gros Morne at sunset, the sky above and immediately around them crimson in the west and clear. Simultaneously, ominous, darkening clouds began slowly rolling in from the northeast. Flashes of lightning stood out blazing against the backdrop of those marmoreal hills and the falling night. Amanda stood on the bridge of the lodge and looked in both directions, waves of peeling thunder in the east, in the west a fullness of blended colors. Nevertheless, even in the thunder she listened in awe to the stillness all around her and felt the uncluttered immensity of what she was seeing for the first time.

Philip was bringing her to a place of such beauty she would someday also come to know intimately as her own.

~ ~

Big Al, as the outporters called him, assembled all the families in Cape St. Charles, Harbour Deep and along the coast. Ever since his birth, he had been a bay boy and the folks up and down this shore knew him as one of their own.

In the face of the fishing crisis, he and the nurses from the Grenfell nursing station mapped out their future defiant stand against the towering bureaucrats and politicians who stood with the powerful and the wealthy. The cod fishery may have collapsed but this harbour community would never.

Rather, Al brought together the cove settlements to draw on the rich resources that have sustained these people for centuries, their music and those songs whose words have come to reflect their lives, their dancing and the food they share, their indomitable courage and faith.

Time passed. His children moved off the Island. Philip, their eldest, went south to the university and then on to the "mainland." Al continued to fish and occasionally hunt to support himself and Ella.

Before there was just the two of them, Ella, spent her time working the pelts to sew clothes for the young ones. The children had often spent days on the hills around their town filling their empters and bringing home buckets of partridgeberries and blackberries. Blueberries, when in season, remained hers to pick being as they were tender and easily squashed.

In winter while Ella climbed into the net-loft to mend the nets with twine in preparation for spring, Al hunted inland for moose. He always hated the killing, especially the salmon, yet there was no other way.

One early morning in September, Al peered out the front window overlooking the wharf he had worked for some forty years. For many of those years, he had prosecuted his catch inshore with other men from the settlement, taking care always to mind the mother fish.

Berries, Tickles and Saltwater Ice

Years ago and all along the coast, the fishing families of northern Newfoundland and Labrador sang about his courage and victories. Many a lad up and down the coast can tell you how Big Al saved his life and the lives of others over the years and how countless times he had steered the men clear through those ice-infested waters far offshore, as well as inshore nearer port.

When the bay seal came in spring, Al was always first out on the pack ice.

Over these last months, Al lay awake many a night, his mind and feelings confused. These fish are a portion of the sea's harvest, food for their table and that is the only way he knew it to be.

He had hauled these "noble" fish into his flat-bottomed dory and watched too often as they struggled their final hour for breath. Most often Al did not allow this, and slit them to die quickly.

Al had loved the sea all his life, yet even when she gave her favors it remained an unrequited love. The sea rose all too often to become savage and cruel. Al lived through her many hours of awesome fury and merciless contempt.

On the sea he had known fear but never faltered. However today he could not bring himself to board his skiff and set out. Like an insidious malignancy, anxiety and a vague foreboding began to bind him. All last night he had lain awake through the hours, immobilized, dreading the sunrise he had once received joyfully.

Ella lay beside him. She caressed him. He had always loved the way she touched him but tonight he felt disconnected, distracted and impotent.

She made him breakfast but he only drank the coffee.

He knew the signs. Al had seen it a few times in other men who never again went out to sea. Perhaps all had come too close to death too many times so that now they lived, trapped in a crippling fear.

After the coffee, he left the house and walked to the wharf and then strolled listlessly along the land-wash. It was a bit frosty. He spotted a growler floating across the bay and a mist lay over the water.

After a few days Ella called the nurse.

Ian and his wife Naomi had come for six months, initially as relief for the nurses stationed here over a long haul. The nurse midwife, however, did not return from England.

Ian and Naomi never left the island, looking after the islanders now, from births to deaths for some twenty-seven years.

Ian found him out back checking over the komatik. Al would use it to haul firewood over the packed snow as he had earlier, hunting for moose, rock ptarmigan and hare – staples for the long winter.

Ella saw them sitting together by the woodpile talking. The two men had been there now for the better of two hours.

Meantime, Naomi dropped by for tea. She and Ella had developed a close friendship soon following the couple's arrival to the cove years before. Both families had three children. Five were living on the mainland, one son of Naomi's, a surveyor, had his house in St. John's.

"Philip's just married and is coming 'ere with his new bride, to be remarried at home in de church on de' hill where he been christened as a baby."

"We just couldn't make it," she told Naomi, "so now de're coming home. Philip told us that he an' Amanda wanted to spend d'er honeymoon 'ere on de island. It was first her idea, he says, to have de service again so Al and I could be here wi'd our friends. Most folks hereabouts know Philip."

Ella turned to Naomi, smiling broadly, "and you were his midwife, and see'd 'im grow all de's years."

The people of this outport did what Newfoundlanders do all so well. The women picked the lush berries and planned the baking, while the men went hunting. The day of Philip and Amanda's arrival and wedding, from every house in the cove and from dozens more along the shore, the rising aroma of fresh bread, pies and cakes mingled with the savoury smells from the roasts and gravy of rabbit, caribou, bear and moose. Some brought in their preserves, an old fisherman from down shore had even brought in several dozen salmon and a few Arctic Char. Another stayed in the community hall and tuned the fiddles.

Al brightened when Philip came down from Martin's plane. He had brought them to the island cove. Nevertheless, following the warm greetings, the hugs and kisses from mother and the children thronging the couple, Philip noted that Al seemed to withdraw from his first greeting and now stood apart, looking off into the distance. He seemed suddenly worried and walked shuffling and with a bent gait Philip had never seen before, his shoulders slouched slightly forward.

He and Amanda followed up the pathway to the house. For him, the sights and sounds of village life and home, and every rock protruding on the path, the bay, the hills rising above and behind the houses, all were so very intimate and familiar. To Amanda, however, this was very new, particularly the genuine warmth of the community who had this day all come together to celebrate with her and Philip, none of whom she had ever met. Even through the impressions of these first few minutes, Amanda realized life was certainly lived differently here than in the urban centers that were once her home.

The ceremony was held in the small white church that had remained a pillar of strength and centre of hope for this community through decades, even centuries, of hardship. For years, the building had been left against the harshest of winters.

Nevertheless, over time people of the settlement renovated it. The altar stood at the front and behind an original stained glass window, and for most of today's Service the sun shone directly through it, its light deflected by the cross.

Following the service, everyone came to the community hall now dominated visually by a homemade feast spread throughout its length.

As the last child came to the table to pile on some blueberry muffins, Philip, a true son of this cove, came forward.

Philip began by saying how buoyed he was, and so very grateful by the spontaneous outpouring by this community of Newfoundlanders that still, to this very day, he remembers as his home.

"I'd been gone a long time," he said, "and having come back here today, this time with Amanda, it is as though I had never left."

He continued: "You share on these vast and lonely shores a proud and ancient heritage – it was God who gave it and it is He who has kept you all these the years, and He will keep you now no matter what the outside world and the government has thrown at you, and might yet."

Philip turned to his parents to remember scenes from his childhood, the tranquil evenings bundled in his mother's homespun shawls, watching

Al carve by the wood stove transforming pieces of wood into the perfect figures of seal and bear, of a fisherman or an Atlantic Fulmar- and such were their gifts. Philip proceeded to unwrap an ivory dog team pulling a komatik his father had once carved and given him for Christmas. "I was seven on that day.

"You were a sensitive and a gifted artisan, Dad, and still have it in you. When we walked in the house today, one of the first things I saw was the caribou you had finished just last night. It is so life-like Dad and obviously carved by someone who feels the land and loves it.

"I have so many memories of the warf and twine loft, Dad where you used to build your boats and kept the traps and nets. In winter there were nets strung from one end to the other. I used climb up to help you mend the holes. You would attach them to a wall and knit with the bone twine needle and card and when you went for a break I would do it by myself, putting a mesh or two in the net. Later you would quietly mend the other holes I had made.

"I remember when the days got so cold the boards of the loft would creak. The inwinds, screechers we called them, so blustery you hung them up, nets and even traps, in the kitchen and knit them there.

"We all remember the kitchen in those days, the smells of the sea and Mom's home-baked bread, all of it mingled together!"

Philip turned to Al, his voice choked with feeling, "I have such fond memories of being there in the loft with you, Dad.

"You have shown me how it is to grow up secure and by your example to walk proud, proud to be who I am, a sea-loving Newfoundlander..."

After the dinner came the fiddles and accordion. At the onset it was the "stomping" with Tommy on spoons that shook the community hall.

The wind that first came up and swept around the cove did not go unheeded.

Newfoundland and Labrador have been the land of wind since time immemorial and the folks dependent on the land and the sea for their livelihood have that intuitive sense of immanence. They see the signs, and they saw them before Martin left for the north Labrador this afternoon. Outdoors, sea birds had come into land earlier in the day, and the fishermen sensed it as a warning. Inside the nursing station the barometer fell slowly and steadily since early afternoon. Nevertheless, in the merriment no one had taken notice nor had anyone listened to the radio foretelling the storm moving across the Labrador Sea.

The sound of the fiddles fell silent and a sudden hush crept through the room.

Amanda had watched the storm gather that first night in Gros Morne. Then she watched and listened in wonder. This evening, however, she felt the tension of a celebrating community suddenly vigilant, a people living at the edge of the sea who knew firsthand that this was not just another storm straying over from Greenland.

The late afternoon grew very dark. No one had turned down the lights in the little white church that now appeared as a lighthouse set on the hill above and behind the school. The cross on its steeple was still alight as the early darkness fell.

The men came out of the hall running down to the flakes and stages to secure whatever they knew the gale would cast about. The rain came in torrents driven hard, painful and cutting to the eyes of the men. Lightning forked across the sea and became the only light, though virtually lethal, for the men scrambling on shore. Some lanterns had blown out and most of the flashlights fell into the bay while they tried to double fasten their dories and boats.

Amanda felt frightened. She had gone out onto the bridge of the hall. Back on the mainland, in the city there are structures, streets, lights, buildings, 911 and sirens. Here on this austere coast, however, the people are alone with their intuitiveness and bravery that must withstand this harshest of nor'easters alone.

Amanda felt suddenly isolated and helpless, *as if I am lost in an open space, and there is no one to call for help*, she thought. Looking around very little remained visible.

The near deafening sound of the wind and lashings of rain, and the thick, low overhang seemed to erase anything even vaguely familiar or safe.

Amanda saw no one, heard no one. Philip had run down to the wharf with the other men.

For a brief moment Amanda felt disoriented and knowing the wide-openness of the land and sea frightened her, except she did see the cross, now somewhat blurred by the rain, behind her on the steeple and the church still alight though only half visible.

That brought the troubling thought of Martin on his way north. Philip requested him to stay for the wedding and dinner. Had he done so, Martin would not be up there, alone, somewhere in his plane.

Amanda shivered.

She turned to go back indoors. Ella and six of the women remained to clean up and keep the soup on while most had gone home with their children.

Ella thought it was time for tea and wait for the men.

"D'ey'd be back soon enough," she informed Amanda, who was still trembling.

Amanda sat down with her new mother-in-law. The others came. A young boy of seven approached Amanda shyly, and soon leaned against her lap. She placed her arm around him. The boy felt warm, in an embracing way, comforting.

In the plain sincerity of the women here, their quiet, calm hospitality to Amanda dispelled her insecurity.

The young boy's mother, Vivian, seemed Amanda's age and like her son, she too was well freckled, her face unstudied, her smile warm.

Vivian's grandparents came here to the Labrador from south Ireland and stayed to fish. "Fish in dose days'" she said, "were plentiful, long before de cod got scooped out. My husband's gone to de mainland, to Toronto. D'er was work he could do. But our son, Jamie 'ere, takes it some 'ard without 'is Dad."

Down by the wharf the men slipped and fell hauling everything up on shore. While some pulled the ropes, the others waded into the ice-cold bay waist deep to help push the boats onto the shore against what had now become an implacable battering.

One of the men lost his footing. It was young Daniel who could not swim. In a split moment the boy had disappeared into a sea of blackness. Once in the water he proved too light against the waves and their draw-back. The undertow dragged him past the strouters on the seaward end of the wharf.

Lightning opened up the darkness of the bay for two brief seconds, just long enough for Al to see the boy clinging to a sunker temporarily exposed by the waves. He ran fast the length of the wharf and jumped into a dory. He seemed to untie her from the strouters as he leapt. Al worked the paddles hard against all odds to reach him. No one on shore saw him or the boy until another streak of lightning flamed across the bay. At that instant they spotted Philip in the water swimming behind his dad.

The men reached the rock together. It took both of them to pull the boy off and into the boat. He appeared fully conscious yet immobile and unable to speak, shivering intensely. The force of the waves carried them to shore and once there, Philip and Ian both knew the immediate danger of hyperthermia. They laid the boy, Daniel, on a makeshift stretcher and carried him carefully up the hill to the clinic.

Philip stumbled and fell up the stairs semi-conscious.

By the time Amanda and Daniel's mother came running in, both the boy and Philip had been started on warmed intravenous fluid and oxygen.

~ ~

The inlet lay sculpted into the coastline. It was a quiet place. Susan loved it, and here she spent many of her leisure hours reading, or writing those belated letters. Often, however, Susan sat on her familiar boulder looking bemused and dreamy out across the tiny cove to those islands she had, for years now, thought to explore one day.

Weather reports predicted a powerful east in-wind with pelting rain. It was forecast for late afternoon and near the time Martin was expected to fly into camp.

For the present, however, the late morning tide rippled in gently towards shore. Pulling her kayak up out of the water, Susan secured it, as she had always done, behind the wonted shore boulder just out of the water's reach.

In the enveloping silence of this place she felt the rhythm of the near-imperceptible stirring of the water. Many-hued stones and pebbles from a bygone eon rolled gently beneath the surface around her bare feet.

Scraping the sea bottom while floating south, icebergs have left varie-gated deposits that, by currents and tides, add their beauty to the slowly yet ever-shifting north shore.

With her feet now out of the numbingly cold water Susan leaned back against the boulder and allowed the warmth of the sun and the cool fresh-ness of the sea air to lull her into a much-needed sleep.

Suddenly roused, Susan woke, alert. She listened intently, yet heard nothing behind her. Someone was watching her. She knew it, and felt the intrusion. Everything remained still, and the water kept up its gentle rhythm beneath her. Susan turned her head slowly. A half stone's throw behind the boulder against which she was leaning, there he was, a lone Labrador Timber Wolf, she thought. He continued to gaze at her unmoving.

Her initial fright turned to wonder. The moments seemed endlessly frozen in time as they both stared at each other. The wolf slowly raised his body and as he did, Susan became aware of his enormity. His was a hand-some and commanding presence.

The wolf moved towards her, falteringly yet towering slightly above. Susan sat very still watching him. It was all so quiet. He stopped and sat, still watching her intently, and she him. He moved his front left paw as if towards her. It was then she noticed the coagulated blood and something sharp and foreign embedded deeply into the infected paw.

Susan began to speak softly. Incredibly he seemed to understand her beckoning him to come closer. Now she could easily reach out and touch him. Susan, knowing that she had some antiseptic ointment left over from the night before, stealthily and slowly reached into her pocket. Very care-fully she extended her clenched hand towards the offered paw.

Yes, she was right —a sharp thorn-like object had penetrated deeply into the wolf's paw. He had not been able to dislodge it. To extricate whatever it was, Susan knew that she would be allowed only one swift and deci-sive move.

Susan held the leg immediately above the paw, carefully assessed the injury and decided her move. Clutching the object at the point where it had entered the soft tissue, she summoned her strength and pulled incisively. The wolf's eyes had not left Susan's face. Now with the sudden and acute pain he let out a high-pitched cry and curled his lips in a snarl. Gripped by fear, she nevertheless continued to hold onto the wolf's paw and with another trained motion poured the remaining ointment directly over and into the wound. The wolf jumped back away from Susan.

He limped away a short distance and lay down to lick his wound. Following several minutes he rose as if to leave, turned and came towards Susan. Again he lay down, closer this time, and continued to watch her.

Realizing what had just transpired between them, Susan began to cry softly.

After a brief while she took out the correspondence paper from her shoulder pack and continued to write one of those overdue letters, aware of the wolf's presence nearby. His eyes never left her. She loved the closeness of this beautiful creature and quietly expressed her gratitude for these inexpressible moments in time given her.

The hour passed. Susan looked around. He had left as quietly and imperceptibly as when he first came. She closed her eyes to savor the freshening wind and hear the lapping of the water. She felt an emptiness, a loneliness…

~ ~

Early that same afternoon, Martin had flown Philip and Amanda from St. Anthony. Because of an emergency run to Mary's Harbour and return, Martin landed them just an hour short of the wedding. He still had a longer flight north, hopefully ahead of the storm.

He flew around the east end of the Mealy Mountains intending to fly along the coast. An impending storm was reported as coming in from north Greenland across the Labrador Sea. The weather station in Kangerlussuaq, Greenland declared the winds to be fierce and erratic. All flights to and from the airport were cancelled.

In half an hour lashings of wind hit him starboard, followed shortly thereafter with a downpour rendering visibility nil. Martin turned windward and climbed higher from two thousand feet to four all the while holding contact with the nurses stationed in Makkovik, then Hopedale.

Martin was very well acquainted with the land and the lakes now invisible below him. Attempting to land on one of those lakes to wait out the worst of it would certainly be risky. To land on the ocean at this point would be fatal. Once down, Martin would likely lose control and the plane, capsized by this storm of wind and sea, would be battered apart against the rocks on shore. To be thrown into the frigid north Atlantic, alone and with no further radio contact, was not an option.

With sufficient petrol remaining, Martin strapped on the survival pack and decided to push on further north. Gradually the downpour changed to a blinding blizzard as he drew close over Nain. Martin knew where he was, but could not land. On land and over the water visibility remained nil.

Word of his situation had carried forward by radio-telecommunication from Hopedale to Nain, and from Nain the message arrived for the nurse at camp. Susan tried to reach him. There was no response. As he flew over Nain no one could hear him; no one could see him.

Martin was alone, dense blackness surrounded him. He listened intensely for any change in the sound of the engine. He knew by instinct that he would be over the camp in less than an hour, the outer limit, he thought, of flying time remaining. Land he must. The fuel had inched much lower on the gauge.

That time now passed. He became certain of having made a terrible misjudgment. Time seemed to stretch on interminably. Without expecting any contact, Susan's voice suddenly crackled loudly through his radio.

"The men have placed flares around the lake to guide you in. There's no ice on the lake… we are praying for you, Martin… look for the flares… Martin, look for the flares… I love you… Susan."

Martin realized his extreme danger. To navigate the storm was one thing, but the petrol gauge measured empty. He circled as much as possible so as to land windward. He began his final descent. Martin hung on, his hands, clenched in fists around the steering. He knew the land, but could not know the precipitous and unforeseen shifting winds. They attacked and the plane shuddered as if convulsed. He watched the altimeter.

The plane came in perilously low over the camp. Martin knew of a slight rise ahead and maneuvered accordingly. He could not see it. From over the crest of the hill he spotted the first flare and in an act of absolute trust, Martin lowered the plane. Its pontoons hit the water. The engine sputtered empty and shut down.

Later that evening, through the candle-lit stillness inside her tent, Susan listened to Martin speak about the meaning of this land and its animals to his people, the Inuit. Their attitude to the land, the polar bear, the fish, caribou and seal, and the whole of creation has been reverential.

"The hunt is not only the basis of our survival," he continued, "it creates a bond between the Inuit and the animal, who has given up his life to preserve the other and this view makes life possible in so harsh an element. Often the hunter prays to the Great Spirit for the animal he is about to kill, or has killed, thankful for its life poured out and food provided.

"The seal gives up and surrenders his life to the hunter who in turn gives freely to his own family, and every household is invited to come and share. All and everyone lives interdependent. This relationship is said to be sacred and has been indelibly forged through a great many centuries.

"To contravene this interdependence, or to pollute the land, or kill more than is needed whether in bravado or commercial greed, is held to be a profanity, reflecting an attitude that eventually leads to a certain communal death.

"Most western people," Martin went on, "outsiders, tend to see the environment and nature as something to be grasped. Having his own 'dominion' over the land, he pulls out and gives nothing in return, except perhaps the polluted end result of his plunder, or he kills to extinction – this is an obscenity.

"For us, the Inuit, like the western Indian much further south and in another country, the land was never untapped nor wild but familiar, never fenced-in but free and holding deep cultural and ritual value.

"There is no 'taming' the land in native thought. For me, this type of outsider thinking is an absurdity. The land and its creatures have been given their form and complexity by the Creator and for this they are respected. To us who have long lived by this 'given,' all life is holy, noble and dignified."

By morning the wind had shifted and a soft prevailing wind from the west blew across camp. Martin and several families looked east over the sea and spotted a rather large number of seal ice-napping. The nights had become quite cold and there was now only a small amount of seal oil remaining to heat the tents. Furthermore, Susan needed a sufficient amount available for the infirmary.

A group of men and boys slid into their kayaks. In a few minutes nine shots rang out and echoed against the hills.

Martin walked down to the narrow lake to inspect his plane still fastened to the shore-line. Susan came and stood high up on a granite outcrop overlooking the lake. The ground on both sides of the path teemed with patches of mixed Arctic evergreens, black spruce, and deciduous shrubs, ferns and mosses. All of these contrasted to the seemingly barren slopes of the Torngats further north.

Earlier in the week Susan was taken into another one of the spectacular fjords that separate these mountains, passing on the way several incised valleys and massive cliffs that rise abruptly out of the sea. To her the silence became awesome. Martin knew of a river in one of these valleys rich in Arctic Char.

Yet now from high on the outcrop she watched Martin. Susan knew that she loved him. The night before she had confessed it loudly into Martin's radio set. Later, she whispered it softly…

~ ~

Martin waited most of the following day for a tank of petrol to be carried from North-West River. When it did arrive, he flew Susan south to Nain and from there on to St. Anthony. Susan was requested to attend a conference. An orthopedic team arrived from Sick Children's Hospital in Toronto.

Isabelle had purchased a house in a small section of town, a few hundred metres away from the new Lighthouse Restaurant overlooking the North Atlantic.

The sunset became ineffably spectacular while she and Susan walked up the road to eat at the old lighthouse. Later, the friends talked their hearts out into the night until they both fell asleep together on the couch.

She had told Isabelle about her time with Laura and in particular the "Yes, I do" answer made by her half a year ago now, and again last night to Martin. During her week with Laura, and in the tensions of that evening, Susan realized unequivocally that she loved Martin. Last night at camp they decided to marry.

Berries, Tickles and Saltwater Ice

~ ~

Susan sent a letter to Laura about her intention to marry Martin by autumn. Also in the letter she mentioned Isabelle.

...She works here and has purchased a house near the mouth of the bay. That first Friday in her house and after she arrived home from work, the neighbors began knocking on her door bringing gifts — three freshly killed rabbits, cleaned salmon, two lobsters that crawled around the kitchen for hours, a pot of seal stew, and a loin of caribou.

Thankfully, Margaret and Sandra from next door stayed behind to help. The first thing, of course, was to phone across the bay for a small freezer.

The neighbors brought Isabelle their family recipes on how to prepare all this. She now even bakes her own bread and fishcakes. It's impossible to buy bread up here following freeze-up.

Isabelle and I have become very close friends, Mother, and I have requested her to be my maid of honor.

I so love my life here...

Some weeks later she received a letter from Laura informing her that the boy, Llewellan, had died. The family intended to come to Raleigh and Burnt Cape on the Northern Peninsula. This is where Cynthia's aunt had lived.

Laura further asked Susan whether she knew Philip... *He recently married here in the church on campus and was presently in Newfoundland visiting his family.*

In that same letter Laura wrote that he had been such a comfort to her the morning Richard died, that she had sat with him on a bench by the river never before having laid eyes on him. *I spilled everything. He was such a comfort to me, yet he said hardly a word. Then I left to check on your plane. I never saw him again when last week I recognized his picture in the paper...*

There was not a mention of Susan's intention.

~ ~

News came in that Philip had been medivac'd to St. Anthony after the storm. An EKG done in the nursing station the previous night revealed a pre-existing irregular heart rhythm accentuated by the hypothermia.

Susan immediately sent back a letter to Laura stating that Philip was admitted to Intensive Care and went on to explain the circumstances.

Two weeks later Laura wrote back,

Your 'life in the north,' as you call it, is just a fantasy, Susan, that I pray fervently will soon evaporate before you make an irreparable mistake. It's a blessing your father is not here…

The letter arrived the same day Isabelle flew in to spend three days with Susan. They sat together near one of the stages where several of the men were cleaning their morning's catch.

"My mother is still so intent on structuring my life around her," Susan commented as she handed the letter to Isabelle, her voice tinged with frustration and mounting anger.

"When I was in secondary school she even tried to orchestrate my dates, and just to structure her safe little world with me in it. Oh, so often I hated ever going home.

How can she ever accept Martin? She has always rejected my friends.

"My mother expects nothing to shake the tight little box that contains her world – all will then remain right and proper, no surprises, no misadventure. That's not me!

"I invited Mom to the wedding. Martin arranged everything, the tickets, where she can stay, everything, even to meet her at the airport in Gander.

"She has not picked up the telephone to answer my calls, nothing.

I supposed I should feel grateful – all she would harp about are those 'missed opportunities' yet again."

Later towards evening, while Isabelle placed a CD in the player, Susan re-read her mother's letter. It fell from her lap.

With the restatement of the aria from Bach's monumental Goldberg Variations her CD finished, the only sound came from three or four Inuit children running and kicking a soccer ball past her open window.

As sunset emblazoned the bay below them in resplendent hues, they sat together as the freshening sea breeze quenched the candle still alight from dinner.

~ ~

Philip's recovery remained guarded. The time he spent in the water that early evening of his wedding day initiated a cardiac crisis from which he had almost died.

During his time of hospitalization, Amanda was invited to stay with Isabelle. Word of Daniel's deliverance and Philip's role in it had spread through town and Isabelle's home was again inundated with food, crawling and dead, best wishes and prayers. Some just came around to meet the girl who had just married this brave son of the coast. Many remembered his father.

In the beginning there were times Amanda felt frightened at the stillness, and the openness. Now, however, while in the strong Newfoundland coastal winds she felt herself wrapped up as if in a protected secret place. It was in here where she could allow herself to safely remember and find no need to disconnect from those intrusive and intense memories of living constantly vigilant against the prowling intent of the man her mother had insisted she call father.

Her memories from home that for a time tormented her nightly, had now lost their intensity. This movement became particularly plain after Amanda began to forgive her mother, and Roger. There had been times she had been too bruised to speak about it, or to pray any further.

Again Philip brought her back to those ancient Psalms, those portals of prayer, confessions really, by which the faithful in every generation have brought all their pain, anger, doubts and confusion, and their gratitude – things that matter most – to their ever-present God. Amanda felt these affections most inclusively.

In the brief time Amanda had spent on the coast, she came to know this yet unfamiliar place to be home. She loved Philip and he loved her. In that assurance Amanda knew herself embraced.

This community in which Amanda found herself was not only different from where she had ever lived, but cleansing and healing. She could dip into any stream and lake to drink freely from its waters. These people of the coastal north adopted her as one of their own as openly as did Philip's parents the day she arrived for the wedding.

There was also her evening walk to Fisherman's Point, most often with Isabelle. Standing there on the cliff and braced together against the wind, the salty sea-spray felt refreshing against their faces. Standing on this spot, she drank it all in as if it would be her last time to this shore.

Martin flew Amanda and Philip home. All had waited for Philip's discharge from hospital. All had waited for Philip's discharge from hospital. While the folks from the community walked down to meet the plane, Amanda's new friend Vivian, whom she met on the evening of the storm, held back and stood on the bridge of her home looking downward onto the bay to where Amanda and Philip had landed.

As the crowd came near the house, Amanda moved away from the others and walked to her friend standing alone. She and Vivian hugged in silence. Her friend's eyes filled with tears, yet she said nothing.

Amanda took her hand. Both sat down in silence.

An idle soccer ball rested against the large rock next to the path.

After several minutes, Vivian wept and her body shook in spasms of grief. Amanda held her friend. Without a word spoken and her friend leaning close against her, Amanda discerned the reason for Vivian's wracking torment.

David Robert was not coming home – ever. He had written his letter in pencil and it arrived from Calgary the day before yesterday.

Vivian rose and went into the kitchen. Returning, she handed the letter to Amanda.

"'e says 'e met someone 'e says 'e should have met years ago," Vivian said almost inaudibly, her words whispered and broken by gut-wrenching sobs.

"D'er's plenty of folks der to help ye and de boy, he says...Not coming back, 'e says, me an' Darcy are 'living out west,' 'e wrote. 'I'm not enough for 'im anymore, 'e says."

Amanda's chest ached. She and Vivian sat together on the bridge steps to the house for the longest time.

Hot tea and fresh pastries awaited the crowd as they led Philip into the community hall where in weeks previous he and Amanda were given just such a reception.

Almost immediately after Amanda left the group to join Vivian on her bridge, talk centred on "Bobbie's" desertion.

"He always was an 'ardened ticket who chased de skirts, and never belonged to de coast. She tried to get him to marry her manys de time but he kept stalling her off."

III

Ilulissat Ice Fjord, West Greenland

Dressed in a thermal suit Susan climbed into her kayak and skimmed toward the leeside of the nearest island. The sea was calm and the early evening crisp. This had become her way of jogging and for clearing her thoughts. In these last few days, feelings of anger and disappointment resurfaced. There were moments of flashback in which she remembered and seethed. Laura's intransigence and prejudices bit in sharply.

A colossal iceberg floating south from Ellesmere stood erect in front of her in an awesome and imperious silence.

She sensed danger. With some distance between, Susan faced it with the bow of her kayak.

Suddenly, breaking through the intense silence around her, it began as far-off thunder. The berg began to roll. It heaved and groaned. Huge chunks of ice broke off violently and disappeared in a frenzy of water. Wave after wave erupted and foamed up from its base and moved towards her. The thunderous response grew ever louder, then waned, and then again in repeated deep, heroic crescendos it began again.

For a while she held her kayak steady. Water rained over her; ice bits were thrust against her. White water billowed under her. She became overpowered. Unbalanced, she rolled over. Undersea everything seemed chaotic. The heaving waters threatened to hold her under, burying her in an unfathomable and churning darkness. She could see nothing. With an all-powerful effort Susan regained control and flipped her kayak so that she was again right side up on the surface. Immediately the turbulence smashed her. Again she turned over.

The seething tumult sounded as if she were enveloped by thunder, peeling and resounding off the Torngats. Susan clung to her paddle. Again she righted herself. She became winded yet struggled against the churning to turn her craft. Susan had to turn it. Her bow must face the iceberg and the direction of turbulence.

Then as quickly as it began, the great berg slowly began to settle and as it did hundreds of ice fragments floated around her. Susan began to shake.

One of the Mounties standing on shore saw what was happening. Along with two Inuit standing next to him, he jumped into an outboard motor boat and sped to the scene. Everyone heard the great berg roll before they knew Susan had paddled out of the bay. Those who had heard came down to the shoreline as the three men sped past.

When the men arrived, Susan turned to give them a half-enthusiastic wave. Still trembling from fear and shivering noticeably, she broke into one of her usual disarming smiles.

"Cool, don't you think?"

There was a moment's silence. The men all smiled broadly as they pulled her alongside.

~ ~

Again, Susan wrote a letter to her mother. The wedding was now three weeks away. Martin had to fly into central Newfoundland and while in the south mailed it. It was an appeal for Laura to reconsider her up to now refusal to attend the wedding.

Underlying her resistance was a disappointment. "I think she feels that I've betrayed her." In Laura's last letter she had berated her daughter again in that common refrain used about Susan "wasting herself" and "we having sacrificed for you over the years."

Dear Mother:

I am very sorry that you feel so strongly towards my decision to make my life here on the Labrador and in my choice to marry Martin. Both of us would love for you to attend our wedding and be with us on our special day. You have by now the invitation, and arrangements are prepared should you change your mind. However, I must frankly say that you really hurt me. Your last letter was completely unfair, and I might add also cruel. This is my honest feeling Mother, and perhaps I should have been more straightforward with you all along.

I want to tell you a bit about my life here. When I first arrived, several years ago now, I had little experience, really I had none, beyond a week's orientation the Grenfell Mission gave us about what to expect on the coast, about the people, their lives and the emergencies we would inevitably face, the sleepless nights checking hourly on someone in sick bay or nights spent on the cold tundra at sixty below while answering a sick call from someone's home up the coast.

There are two of us nurses at the station. My partner is a quali-fied midwife. One of us takes emergencies in the community or into the area round about, while the other remains here in clinic. My days on the coast are filled with daily routines such as pre-natal and post-natal care and visiting the sick or frail elders in the community, making certain that they are taking their prescribed medications or continuing physiotherapy follow-up.

We are both on call 24/7 and must be prepared for anything that comes in. The clinic is open daily for everything, from infected ingrown toenails, fractures, frostbite, complications regarding someone's pregnancy - yesterday we had an ectopic pregnancy that required immediate transfer into surgery. Someone may come in needing sutures, while another needs a change in a post-operative dressing. An abscess needs to be drained at ten in the morning while by ten o'clock at night a teenager needs to be rescued from a snow bank – he is there either because he has fallen over drunk or drug-overdosed. Yes, as you once expressed your concern to me, there is occasionally domestic violence and sexual abuse here, but these problems rage in the south as well.

Daily we draw blood or request a urine sample following which we complete our own lab work, X-rays, Electrocardiograms, dispense medications and even put on and remove casts. I had never done that one before.

There is nursing escort required for emergencies that must be handled in the hospital two hundred miles south, such as heart attacks, food poisoning, uncontrolled uterine bleeding from a partially separated, or retained, placenta, serious head injuries, acute appendicitis, gunshot wounds, and so forth.

Babies born prematurely need immediate care as they are very susceptible to serious respiratory infections. Their fat supply and glucose are low, and their immune system is easily threatened – consequently, so is their life. We always have on hand resuscitation equipment, suction apparatus and incubators. The infants must avoid heat loss so they can continue to burn calories while in transport to the hospital.

However, in the event of a storm and a plane cannot land they must all remain here until the weather clears enough to land a plane. Blizzards are notorious from St. Anthony all the way down the coast north from here. Our task is to keep everyone stable until they are actually medivac'd. This is where Martin comes in.

Just last Wednesday, a fisherman came in carrying his severed thumb in a handkerchief he had stuffed into his pocket. George was his name. He had cut his thumb off earlier that morning but the fishing was so good, George decided his thumb could wait. We quickly called surgery and hitched George and his thumb a ride on the RCMP plane that was about to take off from the airstrip.

About the blizzards here: last February I was called out to visit a girl with severe abdominal pain. Initially the weather was windy but without blowing snow. In another few minutes, however, a wall of snow engulfed me as it was blown about by a bone-chilling wind. I became completely disoriented for what seemed hours. Thankfully, someone from town spotted me, somehow, in between gusts, and pointed me to my apartment. I had only moved twenty or thirty feet, but was lost. This is how many people die in the north. The next morning the girl with acute abdominal pain was medivac'd. The hospital is still treating her for a ruptured stomach ulcer.

On a much lighter note, one of the sounds I love up here is to walk on the frozen and frigid snow. When there is no wind the echo my mukluks create is like no other. Last winter my skidoo broke down in the middle of a lake. Sitting there so quietly I could hear tiny ice crystals skim over its snowy, glacial surface. Next to the time Martin and I sat in the fjord, it was the most profound silence I have ever heard.

In a morning late last March a young man began walking to the small schoolhouse. He was one of the elementary school teachers recently arrived from Toronto and quite unprepared to live in an environment this isolated. He became rather outspoken about missing the noises and the rush of the city.

Having read the orientation booklet that the school board in Nain had forwarded to him months previous, he dismissed their cautions, what he called their "primitive fears."

They never found him. The wind had moved the ice field. Someone did find his cap. It had frozen in the ice some distance from the freshly opened water.

Last week, we had a barbecue. There were some Inuit Elders, two RCMP officers, several teachers and their families, a visiting ophthalmologist from St. Anthony, Martin, and the two of us. We had caribou steaks with sautéed mushrooms, gravy and French fries, seal meat and fowl. I had baked muffins that we ate fresh from my oven. Nathan, one of the constables, brought his guitar and we sang and sang. It was all so "cool"- and the northern lights came and topped off the evening, Mother, in their pinks and greens and blues darting across the northern sky...

The north brings people together. We do not so much make friends here, rather they are given. This bunch up here is fantastic. It's important to participate in community life. Last month they held a square dance. We are all mutually dependent, Mother, in some very real ways. If it had not been for that man directing me out of the storm, I may have been badly hurt- or worse.

Oh yes, I must tell you. I am almost fluent in Inuktitut. Nunatsiavut is Inuktitut for Labrador, "our beautiful land."

A month following our wedding, I am attending a two year-long graduate degree course at university in northern outpost nursing, which includes full midwifery. After that we, Martin and I, will return to the Labrador. While I take that course he will be taking further training as a helicopter pilot. During autumn freeze-up and in the spring as the ice begins to melt in earnest, it becomes necessary to fly these rather than fixed winged aircraft for landing and take-off.

I do love you Mother and trust this letter finds you well.

Love, Susan

PS — in the morning: I must tell you — something amazing happened two weeks ago in Francois, a community on Newfoundland's south shore. A group of kayakers arrived in Nain this morning. You may have already heard about it — the National News reported this incident two weeks ago. Wendy, one of the kayakers told me over coffee.

It's related to the hurricane that came up the eastern seaboard leaving a wide swath of turbulent weather in her wake. That storm hit the south and east shores.

Francois is an isolated and very beautiful outport on the south coast and sits around the water's edge of a steep awe-inspiring fjord. A delicate waterfall runs through the centre of this quiet fishing community.

Her people are friendly, generous and genuine. Francois is one of the few outports to have survived the collapse of the cod fishery and the ruthless, shortsighted government resettlement policies. A tiny, white Catholic Church sits on a rock landing above the town, a Christian testament to what has given her people strength to be who they are, and years back to resist the ruthless bureaucratic bullying to scatter them.

A young mother, Liz Durnford, sat at the kitchen table feeding her toddler, Noah. The wind had beat down on this outport for days, a wind to which the people on Francois had become accustomed. Yet this morning it would threaten a catastrophe.

As Liz listened to the storm, the house began to shake, this time violently. Her sister next door assured her that the storm was usual for these parts. However, deep inside of her Liz knew something was different and carried her child over to her sister's house, a house also built on a rock slope overlooking the bay.

While settling her boy, Liz testified: "I heard the voice of God, not so much that I heard Him, but it was a feeling, like telling me to get my Bible from our kitchen table. I ran out and up the front bridge and the house began to quiver more violently. I thought every window would break. I ran into the kitchen and picked up my Bible, then ran back. Shortly after the house collapsed into the harbour below. We lost everything, but God kept me and my baby."

Kim Courtney, the town's mayor, gave Wendy a copy of her response to the newspapers the next day: "It is indeed an example of faith and how we can overcome great odds. We have already collected enough money for Liz and her family to begin rebuilding. From outside Francois, an expeditionary tour company that comes into port quite often, Adventure Canada, has also taken up a collection for a grant. Even though we are small in numbers, like so many other times in my memory, we did pull together in huge ways to show love and support and not stop doing so just because the task was a big one. I feel that it is a form of thinking that is embodied in the Newfoundland psyche, that you have to fight for what you believe in and what you know is right, and even if the fight is going to test your limits and your faith — the Lord will bring you through."

This story, Mother, demonstrates what I have tried to tell you for so long. Life here remains so uncluttered from what I have left behind — a life uncluttered from the pre-occupation with whatever is new and with whatever comes next, or an individualism that has pushed away community, family belonging and deep abiding, genuine faith.

This is a land of ancient roots, a land so unavailable to many, and at times spurned by, many.

Yet it is such a gift. This is a land that allows me the peace and solitude that I may know that quiet centre within me that God alone can fill.

~ ~

One early morning, the Tuesday following Susan's letter to Laura, Lou Ann came to the nursing station. She had begun labour some hour or two before leaving home.

Soon after arriving and on this her fortieth birthday, Lou Ann gave birth to their eighth child. For much of the nine months, Lou Ann had undergone an exhausting and difficult pregnancy, yet left coming to the health centre very late.

Susan had been concerned. Flannery, Lou Ann's husband, was known through the community as having been physically and emotionally very abusive. Lou Ann had denied this.

Numerous times since her arrival in Nain, Susan visited Lou Ann's family who lived several miles inland, out from town. While with the family, she observed Lou Ann to be pregnant and quite weak. The atmosphere in the home felt oppressive and tense.

Furthermore, Susan became aware of a conspiracy of silence that held this family in bondage. Lou Ann spoke very little and the children not at all, neither to her, nor to their teachers. Two of the children seemed to be losing weight, and all five slept off and on through their classes.

They kept to themselves while at school, and were frequently seen clinging to one another physically.

During her time in the nursing station, Lou Ann did begin to speak, at first tentatively, warily. Susan in her turn waited for Lou Ann to trust her, and as she slowly began her story, Susan listened. Lou Ann's newborn baby became a spark by which their relationship opened little by little.

"The two older ones, Sally and Brenda, have 'secrets' and they use this to bully me. Flannery sees this and just laughs… or he stares at me and sneers. I've thought this out to know it but the more I get to know it the more I'm scared."

Early on the third day Lou Ann sat up in a chair nursing her baby. The cool autumn air blew off the bay. It freshened her room. Susan came through the door.

"Last night when we were talking," Lou Ann said almost inaudibly, "I couldn't think of the right words to say but my life feels like someone's hand, there is a hand pressing us down… it's not only that we're poor, we're all too scared to move, or hope for something, or even run away… he said he'd find us and kill us if we tried – so we don't. That is why we can't fly off to St. John's, for protection you said."

"Do you feel like you're in captivity, is that the right word?" Susan asked.

"Yes." Lou Ann began to cry. Falteringly, she continued: "Flannery is a savage brute and evil. He often hurts me… you know where I mean… when he forces me to do things… I feel so violated and ashamed… I ran away from him two weeks ago, fell down and clawed at the moss and rocks, sobbing and my fingers started bleeding… I could scarcely breathe… suddenly I just wanted to get rid of my baby.

"Angela followed me after a while. I asked her if she could help me into town to see the nurse… you, but Flannery had come out a bit later, heard us, came and slapped Angela and threw her to the ground, and threatened both of us."

Susan called the police. They came, bringing a child caseworker with them from the government in Goose Bay. After she had finished interviewing Lou Ann, she hastened out to the house for an assessment of the children living there, and pressing against Flannery's objections for a daily follow-up routine upon Lou Ann's discharge.

Flannery was born into a family that had come to the north shore on the Labrador. No one ever knew from where, or even when. Some thought that they had fled the United States.

He himself was the seventh child and second son. His father, Lou Ann was never told his name, abused their mother, Eva, in any way he chose and she, in turn, emotionally abandoned the children, especially the girls. In the times Eva was pregnant, the other children, boys and girls both, were freely available to him, and Eva, afraid for her life, said nothing.

Flannery refused all schooling and when he turned nineteen Lou Ann came home with him. She was twenty.

The week that Flannery had turned twenty, both his parents drowned. His brothers and sisters scattered far and wide. He never inquired about any of them.

At the time, Flannery fished and cut firewood for whoever would buy from him. Only a few ever did. He remained estranged from the community.

Flannery controlled the family through intimidation, fear, and threats directed at them yet often involved himself, as he said once, "to show you I am the victim."

"I'm going into the bush and shoot myself. I can't live with this noise from all of you," he often yelled.

That is when terror gripped Lou Ann and the children. When Flannery came home, with the favorite double-barreled shotgun saved for these occasions, everyone tiptoed quietly for the remainder of the day.

One bright afternoon in midwinter, Lou Ann telephoned the nursing station explaining that Flannery had again headed for the bush.

"He's been real quiet and sullen lately, likely because the case-worker comes every day. He never speaks to her. Flannery hasn't gone to the bush for a month.

"But this afternoon," Lou Ann observed, "he seems different. He seems to be brooding more, especially after she leaves. Before he walked out a while ago, I was breastfeeding Darleen. That's another thing that just makes him so angry."

Susan assured Lou Ann that she would be over in forty-five minutes and bring Kimberly, the other nurse in the station. "There's been a snowmobile accident. The boy is bleeding heavily and has a broken leg. Following that we will be right over."

It was four o'clock and school had been out for an hour.

In another half hour she and Kimberly put on their snow rackets and crossed the harbour. Taking off the rackets in the back driveway, they leaned them against the house and walked up the bridge stairs. As was customary, Susan opened the back door.

As they came into the kitchen, there was a very loud blast. Before Susan spotted Lou Ann she watched as Flannery's now headless body stood, as it seemed in mid-air, then twist and fall in slow motion, fresh blood being spurted out in all directions. The gun had already hit the wood floor. His head, now a deformed mass of bleeding tissue remained stuck to the cross beam. Turning to her right, Susan saw Lou Ann and all the children, save a boy in grade eight who had gone home with a friend. They had been lined up by Flannery to see and hear their father "say goodbye," as he said before pulling both triggers.

The infant remained on the breast, Lou Ann and her children, all of them staring ahead. She seemed paralyzed, then slowly vomited over her child. The children began to scream hysterically...

For the first time in her young life, Susan witnessed an incredibly destructive evil tear into the lives of a mother, and to all her children who were bullied to watch and hear, and who now will have a permanent vision of what happened forever branded on their minds, spirits and bodies.

Susan wrote to her friend the next evening,

... in a time like yesterday, the peace that permeates this land, of which I wrote you previously, seems very fragile. This event has left me shaken, and indeed disturbed. Actually, I felt physically sick, certainly very nauseated.

After the shooting and dealing with this terrible crisis, we called for the mission plane. It was Martin who came straightaway and flew Lou Ann and the children to St. Anthony. We couldn't talk openly. There was so little time, and our priority was to get the family out. Kim escorted them, while I crawled into my bedroom and just broke down. Thinking about the children, and Lou Ann, what will now happen to them, and much later, what a horror to remember! A very, painful case of post traumatic stress will, I am certain, torment them for years, probably forever. It was their own father who held them up in front of himself and carved this now intractable torment into their little hearts! I cannot fathom the horrific depths of darkness into which Flannery had sunk to even imagine such an irrevocable deed.

I do know a little of what it is to be emotionally distant from those I love – yet I have never experienced brutality or invasive vigilance, neither the anguish nor the hopelessness in which no one ever came to expect anything else from one another. In Lou Ann's family each lived lives brooding and exhausted, "unable to see anything change – ever," as she told me a few weeks ago.

Martin telephoned later but I could scarcely find anything to say. I spent last night unable to sleep, and very tense. With every familiar sound in the building I jumped out of bed. I was afraid to close my eyes, and could not stop shaking - those recurring images flashing back, of seeing the whole thing over again...

Martin flew Kim back this morning and remained with me most of the day. I am so grateful that he stayed…

Love, Susan

IV

The Friar, Francois, Newfoundland South Shore

Two young people who have not yet known one another will meet, and during the course of their relationship, this meeting will set in motion far-reaching influences for each of them.

Thérèse has grown up in a family with two brothers, one a year older, the other younger. Her parents spend much of their time working – he is a forest ranger; she teaches languages and literature at a local college. For as long as Thérèse remembered the three children spent hours, at times days and on a few occasions, weeks alone.

> *At sixteen I left them, walked away really... my older brother Adolph often showed Jimmy how to touch me. That was just the beginning. Then I became scared because they both told me never to tell because my parents 'will never believe you,' they said. I did tell my mother, after I could no longer sleep and when I did sleep, I had disturbing dreams. She yelled at me, called me a liar - and so did my brothers. In the morning mother and dad told me to get out.*

> *Many of the dreams were similar. I was at our high school prom... every girl had a beautiful dress except me. My mother and dad dressed me in a burlap bag. My date was a tall boy with curly black hair. A short time into the evening he gave me messages like I was in the way. I got up and poured some coffee but on the way back to our table someone fell against me and the coffee spilt over my dress. It really hurt so I asked my date to help me. He ignored me and so after a while, I left walking out into the rain alone. I made my way to a small bridge over a creek and sat down.*

> *I stare into the blackness ahead of me, vacantly, never really thinking about anything. It is very dark and I become disoriented, and so I sit there all night. It feels peaceful.*

> *No one ever comes looking for me... and I never know if I ever get home.*

The day Thérèse did leave home, she made her way into the city centre. By dusk she was alone - as Therese had not taken either money or food, she sat quietly on a curb not knowing what to do or where to go, nor even whom to ask. The evening air became cool from off the sea. The uplifting sounds of a Celtic band drifted out from a nearby pub.

A lady and her husband walked slowly past her, turned around and approached Thérèse. It turned out that she was an intensive care nurse and he a veterinarian.

"You're looking a bit chilled, and hungry," the nurse said as she wrapped her own shawl around Thérèse. "Before seeing you we were both thinking of going across the street for a hamburger and whatever. Would you like to join us?"

"There is something very unusual about them," Thérèse thought to herself, yet said nothing to either, just nodded. She got up from the curb, and the three of them moved across the street and into the restaurant.

~ ~

Thérèse had now been at the shelter four weeks. The nurse whom she had met that first night was quite familiar with the home. Thérèse had been admitted after the three of them left the restaurant, given a small comfortable room and a promise that the nurse would call tomorrow afternoon. Her name was Sylvia, and she came to see her every evening.

Thérèse felt uprooted, even homesick for the first few nights, yet knew as well that returning would enmesh her into the sick dynamics, denials and abuse that had ultimately led to her expulsion.

"Still," she said to Sylvia one evening, "I feel so separated from everything."

At another time: "It all felt like I was sinking into the deep waters of death." At still another: "I have these torrents of self-blame, like it was all my fault... guilty feelings come every night... I try to bury them and then I hate myself so much... I cry myself to sleep a lot."

For the remainder of the summer, autumn and then the winter, Thérèse lived and worked on a small farm, picking fruit and berries, making jams and jellies, milking the cows and chopping wood for winter's fires. She warmed to the family and to Jack and Dorothy who had taken her in. Nevertheless, memories of shame, and then anger plagued her quiet days.

As these emotions ripped and shackled her, Thérèse spoke less and less...

"Yesterday morning Thérèse went mute," said the farmer's wife Dorothy to Sylvia. "She cannot speak, or maybe will not – we don't really know."

Behind her long silence, Thérèse writhed, locked in memory and pain. Sylvia knew yet Thérèse said nothing.

Thérèse moved through her days. She ate little, and usually sat stroking Boudreaux, the family's spaniel.

"He often sneaks near her when she sits like that... many the time I would steal a glance her way, and many a time I see a tear or two run down her cheeks. At these times I will go and sit with her beside the fire - that's wood she has cut herself, you know. Jack can't do that no longer."

Sylvia remembered from what Thérèse had once confided, namely, that *Alice in Wonderland* has been her favourite book for as long as she could read – so Sylvia began reading the story out loud, encouraging Thérèse to read alternate paragraphs. Still, she remained silent.

Nevertheless, every other evening Sylvia came, and she read, and together on most of these evenings, they walked along the path leading to the narrow waterfalls, near to where two beaver had backed up the water from flowing along where the creek had once long and freely meandered.

It was Tuesday afternoon, six months on - a light early morning rain had left the ground along the path still damp. A doe and her fawn crossed over ahead of them,

"They're so beautiful," Thérèse whispered softly.

Taken aback, Sylvia ever so slowly turned, afraid to lose this moment, yet whispered, tears now welling up in her own eyes, "Yes, Thérèse, they are."

Thérèse turned to face Sylvia. Neither said another word. Sylvia became afraid in the silence between them, anxious were Thérèse suddenly to panic and draw back.

Sylvia took her hands into hers. Both realized, as if in slow motion, this breakthrough moment; each held on to the other and cried.

~ ~

The bus eastbound arrived in the city port early. The hours and the countryside had sped by swiftly. He was coming home.

The minute Nathan stepped away from the coach he smelled the freshening sea air, and could feel it in his bones. While he still needed to travel several hundred kilometers northbound along the coast, he had to wait. The only ship that would take him nearest home was to leave tomorrow noon.

Although his father was of late too sick to fish on the Labrador, no one in the cove ever expected Nathan to return.

Long desolate months had passed since those days of Christmas last year. That was when he knew that his life had begun to fall apart. At first it seemed to him as though he stood back and watched all the scenes unfold from a distance.

"It's all seemed a disconnect, almost illusory," he thought.

For a long time thereafter everything he tried – it was all an effort just to place one foot ahead of the other. Even his best friend on the mainland backed off – there was just nothing to talk about.

Walking away from the bus station, Nathan found himself in a narrow cobblestone lane that he had once known so well. About to turn into an old familiar English café, his attention was drawn towards a short by-path to his left leading up to a small newly renovated shop, designed as if built into the stonewall that lined the walkway.

He turned, and entered a unique room with a living loft and an adjoining hallway, and this in turn led to a patio out back. On display in the main room were authentic Inuit sculptures from Baker Lake. Carvings from Saint-Jean-Port-Joli in Québec lined the back wall.

A lean man of middle age approached him, tentatively, when a young woman came down, unaware of Nathan's presence, called out to her father crying and speaking in an agitated manner. It became clear that she was the artisan whose pottery was in the pine cupboard into which Nathan was viewing. Her name was Andrea.

Nathan felt conspicuous and intrusive. Embarrassed, he walked out into the patio.

The girl's mother followed him, slowly her hand reached out and touched his bare arm, her eyes raised as if to say something.

"I'm sorry," she said. Her eyes, now filled with tears, fell away from his, her hand still moving softly on his arm. Nathan stood there confused, his emotions in turmoil.

This family, unknown to him until twenty minutes before, had drawn him into their pain, and desperation.

They had initially opened their shop full of dreams and talents overflowing. There were beautiful things to purchase, yet no one ever came in to buy.

He left the shop. Andrea was still standing beside the bureau with the Inuit carvings, now very silent. Her mother's gaze followed him with a look lovely and yearning.

Nathan felt drawn, yet he walked away. He had felt awkward by the obtrusion from this troubled family.

Deeply shaken, Nathan strolled along the river that emptied into the sea. Standing on the water's edge he felt the spray from the relentlessly pounding sea against the shoreline rocks. He loved her as did many a seaman before him. The sea, and in winter the ice groaning beneath him, had become as intimate as any mistress. Being absent from her for so long became a gut-wrenching longing to be near her, to be one with her again in the old family dory with his father, fishing from the pre-dawn morning until late every evening. Coming home, at whatever the hour, his mother always welcomed them with her hot Newfoundland soup and a cup or two of tea, forever grateful to God for His safekeeping.

Nathan was unaware of how long he had stood there remembering home. His memory this morning, standing there, was also bitter.

Feelings and thoughts seemed to force themselves back to the family in the shop. Nathan felt their intractable family pain and their shame of impending failure, their being together and their unbearable aloneness, living their nights in palpable silence and their days in struggle and hopelessness, their years of passionate loving, and now their hunger for the slightest touch. Once they dreamt together of owning an esteemed business – all three were so devoted to art – yet now, insidiously their dreams began eroding until today nothing remained but waiting for the door that the father himself had meticulously carved out of pine, to irrevocably shut behind them.

For Nathan the gate closed behind him, so to say, in a year that was supposed to open up opportunities he never thought would come his way on the coast.

Early in his first semester at college, he met Thérèse, a south-shore girl, blithesome and sociable, a girl some called "Butterfly," whom others thought of as a spoiled brat. She was one of those students who flittered about the party circuit unperturbed by what others said of her, all the while hiding a rage within that never eased.

At a college prom one night in early December, Thérèse had far too much to drink and announced loudly for everyone to hear, "my family has secrets which I now want to tell, just for your ears alone my dearest friends... a secret that I have buried...wait 'till my parents find out I squealed."

Thérèse stood in the centre of the hall and began to laugh hysterically, threw up both arms, her hands as if trying to touch the ceiling, her feet wide apart. She continued loudly, pausing between each word,

"My dad 'imposed himself' into my life, not once, not twice...," she paused momentarily, "but then my younger brother, he too..."

Thérèse stopped, looked about her with eyes wide, yet not seeing. She slowly lowered her face to stare into her hands. Without saying another word, she suddenly sank to the floor, trembling, and began to sob.

The others stared at her anticipating some nightmarish revelation. It was Nathan alone who came to her and remained with her. He danced with her for the remainder of the evening.

Nathan rented a room for them near campus and for a while all was radiance, laughter, and uninhibited passion. Lost in each other's embrace and exhausted, they often stayed home from class, remaining together for days without leaving their apartment.

Unknown to Nathan, Thérèse became pregnant. She slipped out one evening. In the following morning telephoning him about a family emergency, and assuring him of her return by Saturday. He believed her.

Thérèse did not come home until the following Wednesday, very drunk. She offered no reason, and Nathan did not push for one.

Thereafter, an emotional distance wedged itself between them. Their one moment of agreement in the following week came when Nathan suggested that they go out east together, home for Christmas.

This proved an unmitigated disaster.

Nathan's nieces and nephews surrounded the newly arrived couple with noisy voices and running about, their faces filled with obvious fun and excitement.

Then there was Jenny, Nathan's niece, bright, blossoming and ever so pretty. He always thought of her as "my quiet, freckled red-head with the infectious smile." He loved her, and she adored him.

Later that afternoon on Christmas Eve, Jenny approached Thérèse sitting in the old rocker.

"Nathan tells me he likes you a lot, but I don't," Thérèse spoke, no rather rasped, with a finality and a bluntness that was weighed for its effect and deliberate.

Jenny backed up against the far wall, pale and beginning to tremble. Nathan sat unmoving, riveted to the spot – a paralyzing fear gripped him.

Jenny looked to her uncle. He said nothing. Thérèse sneered towards Nathan.

Jenny felt naked, numb, alone and betrayed. Someone broke the silence by suggesting it was time for everyone to stroll over for Christmas Eve Mass. After Service they walked across the harbor to Auntie Gwen's whose traditional meal was known to be the best this side of St. John's.

Unknown to the others, Thérèse walked off somewhere into the cove's piercingly bleak winter night. She stumbled back several hours later, frost-bitten, angry and drunk, her clothes grainted with earth and disheveled. No one knew where she had gone, nor did anyone ask.

Overnight a sadness Jenny had never known overcame her. Nathan looked for Jenny in the morning. He saw her watching from a distance. Jenny looked out the kitchen window as Nathan crossed the tickle and off the island in that early Christmas morning.

For Nathan the memories of that day and night remained in disbelief, dissociated, "out there," and far too painful to own. In the weeks after Christmas a self-loathing came alongside the recurring vision of having left Jenny that night, abandoned and bewildered.

Now almost a year later, and before he headed north, Nathan remembered - and as he remembered the flashback of that evening yet again blazed afresh from his memory. Nathan sobbed his grief and disappointment.

Berries, Tickles and Saltwater Ice

~ ~

Nathan booked his passage north, expecting to leave by midday tomorrow and arrive on the east Labrador early the following morning.

The scent of firewood burning from the kitchen stoves was first to greet him as he walked along the landwash towards the houses. A dense fog had begun to roll in. Several men were standing down next to the old net loft.

At first he did not see her standing on the cliff-rock rising as a breakwater out of the depths of the in-tide beach.

Then he saw her, partly obscured by the rolling in-fog, her long auburn hair ruffled by the morning in-wind. He froze.

She saw him, hesitated for a moment, turned and came towards him waiting for her.

As she came to him her eyes searched his for some recognition of how she, and him, once had something very special together. Upon coming to him still standing quietly watching her, the pain of memory dissolved.

"I've come to see you," he said.

"Not because your dad is sick?"

"Yes, that too." He paused. "I haven't forgotten how I abandoned you. I didn't take your side that night… had to, wanted to come and say I'm sorry Jenny… 'can't know why I didn't come to you, left you later just standing there against the wall… wrote you once but never mailed it."

She moved closer to him now. They were both quiet, searching through the fog for something right to say, Jenny to answer him, again remembering the pain; he not knowing whether to talk further.

"She hated everything I loved. After we left last Christmas I felt lost… didn't belong with her either. It's not the same here."

Jenny understood him to mean things have changed in the cove.

"I'm finishing high school in a year, likely going in for nursing at Memorial."

They walked up from the bay-land slowly, together. Neither spoke. On both sides of the path bright-orange lichens clung like patchwork on surfaces of rock and tree bark. Abundant clusters of scarlet-leaved blueberries

matted the headland as it reached out to the sea. Off shore a sculptured iceberg on its migration floated irresistibly southward.

Jenny placed her small hand in his, a gesture that spoke her forgiveness, her answer to the shame, the deep-felt pain and uncertainty both had felt for so long. Jenny was someone who loved him in spite of it all – and he loved her.

"You've come back in time for the wedding tomorrow," she said. "You know Martin Peter, the pilot for the mission – he's marrying his long-time sweetheart, the nurse from Nain…

~ ~

The morning of the wedding came quickly. Early in the day Martin picked up Susan and his parents in Nain, and Isabelle in St. Anthony. He did so, on his return flight with the minister from Greenland. Martin had given himself three days for the trip with a longer stopover in Ilulissat.

On their landing a phone message arrived from Nain by way of Mary's Harbour stating that Susan's mother had landed in Gander and wondered if anyone could come for her. Susan forwarded a call to Gander Airport reassuring Laura that a plane was on its way.

It did not fizzle anyone knowing that the wedding would now be several hours late. Everyone knew that this was life on the coast. Martin and Philip circled across and south to St. Anthony for refueling.

The clear weather made for an unlimited ceiling. Martin felt on edge. His anger towards Laura had been agitating for some time, not for any dislike or even prejudice she may have towards him, but for the emotional distress her attitudes had had on Susan.

Just north of the airport Martin received clearance to land.

"I'm okay now. You go on and bring Laura out. She'll probably remember you. I'll be checking in with the flight deck."

Martin was relieved with the distraction of walking away and checking weather patterns for the day even though they had been thoroughly reported to him while in flight.

With that Martin disappeared. Philip entered the passenger area. Laura stood in front of the water cooler. Seeing him enter, Laura turned and with a drink in hand met him genially in the centre of the room.

Laura was wearing a full-length dress and carried a rather large, matching handbag. Her hair was cut short. Philip remembered it long.

Philip carried her somewhat sparse luggage to the plane and helped Laura to her seat. Martin had not yet appeared.

She inquired if Philip was to fly her north and whether it would take but a few minutes.

"Your pilot will be right back."

"*I desperately hope so*," he thought. Philip could not bring himself to tell Laura that they were waiting for Martin, the only pilot with the only plane to come for her.

"Susan just flew in from Nain when we received the message that you were here."

"Have you known Martin long?"

"Yes, for about fifteen years. We were at university together – roommates actually."

Martin appeared through the gate doors and walked briskly up to his plane and climbed into the pilot's seat. He spoke a quick and curt hello and began looking over the panel in preparation for take off.

"I'm Martin, and you would be Laura. Very pleased to meet you," he said smiling and turning to look straight at her.

Laura sat motionless, staring at him as Martin started both engines. As they taxied to the assigned runway, he added, "We've a wedding to attend and some very good food to eat. The folks are putting on quite a spread, so let's move and make some noise."

Laura sat as if dazed still staring at Martin as the plane lifted off the tarmac.

As they flew over the Northern Peninsula and along the south Labrador coast, Martin became Laura's personal tour guide. The hour's flight carried them over the terrain he knew intimately and loved to talk about.

Laura heard only some of it until he described the fjords in the Torngat Mountains much further north. Laura gave a start of recognition. She thought back to that evening when Susan revealed to her the feelings she had for this man who was now flying her to the wedding. It was a moment she had been afraid of for so long.

This realization impacted her visibly. He glanced at her sideways.

"Martin…" she stopped her sentence.

"Yes. I really am glad that you have come. You will have made Susan so happy..."

On approach, Martin flew over the island towards the makeshift airstrip on the mainland Labrador. He laughed and pointed to a herd of caribou grazing on the runway. He "buzzed" them once and he "buzzed" them twice and still not one would be frightened off to allow him landing space.

Martin contacted the cove and requested that they come over and scare them from "ground zero." He held and circled for the quarter hour it took the folks to come off the island.

A group of men and children finally ran up to the herd – still not one budged. Martin "buzzed" them a third time. Slowly a few of the herd looked up and seemed to motion the others to move over and free the "runway." At that the caribou ambled about fifty feet off to the side, just far enough for Martin to land.

Susan ran up to the plane. Martin was the first to step down. She looked intently for any sign. Martin smiled.

Philip was on the other side of the plane with Laura. Susan walked around the craft.

"Mother, you remember Philip..."

Arm in arm Susan, already in her wedding dress, led Laura down the path to the water's edge.

Isabelle stood on the bow of the zodiac and reached for Laura's hand. Laura recognized her immediately as the doctor who had been so kind to her on the long, lonely night of Richard's death and who had embraced her on the bench that early morning. She remembered Susan mentioning her in several letters.

All this flashed through Laura's memory while simultaneously all around her there unfolded an unfamiliar and austere landscape and caribou blocking the runway!

Go figure that one, she fretted to herself, *too much, too much. I feel pushed along by it all. Why am I really here?*

As Laura and Susan arrived in the village the lone bell from the church peeled across the outport. Not only was Laura's call earlier so unexpected, but during the time of her flight from Gander, another surprise was waiting.

Martin arranged for a delegation of Susan's friends to arrive from Nain, the very same that had accompanied her to the plane. Unknown to Susan, another Twin Otter had been waiting out of sight ready to load up in an hour following Susan's send-off.

Years were to pass, three children born, yet Susan never asked him how he had pulled that off.

The little white church on the hill was soon overflowing with people. To Laura's surprise Philip escorted her to the front around and over the children excited and scrambled in the aisle.

The new-ness of everything, even the strange-ness, all pressed in on Laura. For the first while she heard little – was it all illusory, surreal, yet the hymn, "I have heard that somewhere. Yes, that is familiar," she reassured herself.

The processional chosen by Susan was the Austrian hymn brought to the Labrador a century ago by the Moravians, *Glorious Things of Thee are Spoken*. Words were printed out in English and Inuktitut and sounds from the mixed chorus filling the sanctuary echoed through the cove and were heard by the crew of a sailing craft just entering the calm waters of the bay.

Laura thought Susan's ivory colored brocade wedding dress very suited considering that she had fallen in the water disembarking the zodiac an hour before. Martin had quickly changed from his casual pilot's garb to a dark suit.

The minister led them through the Order of Service with its prayers and Scripture.

*Who is he that cometh up from the wilderness, leaning upon
her beloved? I roused thee under the apple tree: there thy mother
brought thee forth...*
*Set me as a seal upon thine heart, as a seal upon thine arm:
for love is strong as death; jealousy is cruel as the grave:
the coals thereof are as coals of fire, which hath a most vehement
flame.*
Many waters cannot quench love, neither can the floods drown

*it: if a man give all the substance of his house for love, it would
be utterly scorned. Song of Solomon 8:5a, 6-7*

To Laura's questioning amazement the words read and spoken, and the hymns sung, were very familiar and rooted in her past, years ago back home. Yet she had rarely given much thought "to these things," as she once said.

Seeing Isabelle now kneeling in front of the altar with Susan, Laura remembered their brief acquaintance, circumscribed as it was to a painful night, and a very lonely early morning.

From the moment of recognition in the zodiac an unfolding sense of familiarity, alternated with an unsettling illusiveness. She as yet had no words for it.

As the pastor from Greenland prayed a benediction for God's peace in her daughter's marriage, Laura felt a growing sense of uncertainty, even fear she thought, that threatened to profane the harmony of these moments her daughter long desired to share with her.

"*Here in these alien surroundings, Susan is binding herself to this man, Martin, to love and desire him above all others - and what about me, struggling at home... Richard's gone now,*" she wondered in a whisper to herself. She became aware of a feeling of detachment, as merely a spectator.

"From the minute I landed in Gander, this entire episode was like watching a confusing play, with me somehow in it," Laura recalled days later.

~ ~

Ron and Cynthia stood on the exposed limestone cliffs of Burnt Cape overlooking Pistolet Bay. In the distance lay the south Labrador as the land angled northward.

Aunt Rita had spoken to Cynthia often about connectedness and living rooted to this land, a belonging Cynthia now desired for herself.

Neither spoke for the longest time. The air felt crisp, almost cold. The rocks stacked on top of one another, the rounded steep caves, the Arctic Dandelion and the Fairy Slipper Orchids, the wind-stunted and densely matted tuckamores - they were all there, and all so familiar as if nothing or no one on this land had ever moved. Although known as the Barrens, it has always been her most beloved spot on earth.

Cynthia remembered back through the years as if they were yesterday. Yet so much has happened since the last time she had come, so many feelings, such wasted emotions, so much peace that she had once known here, thrown away, their family having come so close to ruin – and for what? What had she been following these last few years – an illusion, a deception?

She and Ron were remarried, a few weeks before Llewellan died. They all came together with the chaplain and stood around Llewellan's hospital bed. Though ever so sick, he lay propped up on his pillows and watched his parents intently as if wanting to secure every inflection, every nuance, every word, every promise spoken.

The child felt happiness that they were now all together again, yet he also knew, although he did not fully understand, that he was soon to die and would not be there for his birthday. He sensed it, as most children do, before anyone told him.

Slowly, Cynthia had accepted Llewellan's death. She now missed him intensely. Standing there on the barrens so full of life, Cynthia suddenly felt the upsurge of grief pressing against her. Standing there, overlooking the bay, it wrenched at her guts. Her legs crumbled and she fell to the moss under her feet, hands burying her face, sobbing, her body wrenching trying desperately to extricate the pain from some bottomless depth inside. She knelt there crouched over, rocking back and forth, crying and whispering into her drenched and sopping hands, "I'm so sorry... I'm so sorry...O please God forgive me, please... I have wronged the children... why wasn't I there to protect him? Ron... I'm so sorry...O God, it hurts so deep."

Ron sat on the shallow shifting soil beside her, crying, holding her.

~ ~

Vivian and Amanda left the Service early and walked briskly down toward the hall to help with the food layout. Coming around a sweep in the path they could see a sailboat with an outboard motor aftmost on the vessel. The sailing craft was left anchored a short ways out. One man, perhaps two, and a woman in their mid- to- late thirties were seen rowing a small boat to the wharf and tying her to the strouters.

An hour before, Ron and Cynthia had met two fishermen in a dory just outside the bay. Ron had requested information as to the nearest medical facility. Since morning he felt considerably weakened by an abdominal pain and distension, and felt it difficult to walk let alone help sail their boat any further. One of the men then offered to come aboard taking them the remainder of the way into port.

Vivian ran to fetch the nurse from church. Naomi came straightaway. Ian had been called into the surgery an hour earlier. A child and his parents came to the clinic. The boy from down the bay had several fishhooks that penetrated through his cheek.

Once in clinic, Naomi examined Ron. He had been unable to eat since late yesterday, and his bowel sounds were louder than Naomi decided should be normal. Furthermore, he had vomited four times in the boat, and now again. As he did, Ron groaned with pain.

She suspected a serious obstruction that quite likely would require immediate surgery. She called St. Anthony for an airlift transfer and established an intravenous to replace lost electrolytes. Other preliminary diagnostic measures were initiated before the plane landed twenty minutes later.

Within that half hour, people from the wedding began to walk down the pathway. Laura passed the nursing station and recognized Cynthia standing in the doorway.

At first Laura presumed she was on emotional overload. Nevertheless, once Laura became certain that it really was her friend from Kingston, she excused herself from Susan and ran up to the porch.

Cynthia watched Laura coming towards her. She looked at Laura without seeing. Cynthia felt numbed by it all. Yet on seeing her friend climb the stairs and call her name, she felt a sudden relief.

Before either could say anything more, the plane circled overhead. Immediately Ron appeared wrapped in blankets and lying on a stretcher carried by Naomi and Ian.

Philip had remained behind and now took up the front end of the stretcher from Naomi. She and Cynthia ran to the boat and rowed urgently to where the sail yacht was anchored and brought out their several suit-cases, wallets and backpacks.

The plane moved into position whereby Cynthia could easily embark directly from their sailboat. It taxied windward and became airborne within moments.

Laura remained standing on the wharf gazing ahead and amazed while the plane receded beyond the hills.

"Mother."

The call from the upper landing broke into Laura's distraction.

"Come for a few photo shots. Dinner will be ready."

Several minutes previous Susan had heard the plane descending and turned to see a stretcher carried out through the doors of the nursing station and Laura standing there, then moving along with the small group to the wharf.

As the plane faded past the distant islands, Laura sensed Philip watching her, still standing on the spot from where they had lifted the stretcher. He approached her, nudged Laura's arm and together without speaking walked up the stairs and into the banquet hall.

~ ~

Vivian sat on the steps of the clinic that overlooked the harbour. A cool freshening east breeze sent gentle ripples over the water. Young Jamie bent over in the shallow shoreline, searching intently for any piece of ancient volcanic rock, or perhaps even a sculp of glacial rock to be shown at school the next morning. He loved to wade knee deep in the cool water explor-ing for things he had never yet seen, discovering beautiful stones, and sometimes wiggly things, to give his mother.

Jamie often leaned up against his dad's old row dory now pulled up on shore and abandoned. In his pocket he always carried the iridescent piece of Labradorite that David had given him as a Christmas present two years ago. Every time he held it up to the sun, Jamie gazed open-mouthed at the scattering of light that gives off greens and blues on its surface.

He simply could not understand – Vivian told him that his dad was not coming home. Why? It was unreal, a blur – even for her.

Alone, and curled up in bed, the pain of betrayal and profound loss would often nigh overwhelm her. She no longer cried at these times. It just hurt too much. He had really never loved her. Vivian had loved him and given everything, "but I'm just not enough for him." This thought took hold of her, time and again.

She and Amanda had become best of friends. Amanda's love and acceptance uplifted her. As Amanda's father had read to her words and truths from the psalms he loved, she always remembered them, and Vivian drank from them solace and courage.

Amanda explained, "Psalm 55 is a cry to God of a loved one betrayed and afraid, full of screams and violated, distraught beyond comprehension. Nevertheless, though all appears as darkness, this psalm, like all the others, assures us that we do not stand alone."

If an enemy raised himself against me, Vivian read, I could take it. Yet, it is you, my husband; you who have shared my bed; you with whom I have "enjoyed sweet fellowship;" you, David have now become my enemy.

The words from your mouth were smoother than butter, but war and deceit were in your heart; your words were softer than oil, yet were they drawn swords. Give ear to my prayer, O God… my heart is sore pained within me; and the terrors of death are fallen upon me…

Today is Tuesday. The wedding guests, almost everyone from along the coast, north and south, have gone home. Susan's mother flew to St. Anthony just yesterday to be with her friend, and to greet the newlyweds – no one had an idea as to where they disappeared.

Nathan strolled along the path towards Vivian.

She looked up to see him. " How's yer Dad"?

"I'll be taking him to St. Anthony tomorrow. The hospital will give him some tests. Since yesterday he feels a bit better."

"Yer Mom has been holding up real well all Spring. Right glad yer home."

"Dad has managed to bring in enough firewood for the winter. Mom says that a bilk of wood remains piled along the road. By week's end I'll go in, pick it up and start building up enough cords for next year. Gotta get my license in the morning to cut and pile it. Mother has given me her grocery list for tomorrow. Aside from that I'll need to go hunting and bring in a moose, do a bit of fishing… How's Jamie?"

"He's sad a lot. He just can't bring words to't."

Jamie saw Nathan. He ran up to his mother, searched his pockets to lay out his new collection, five or six smooth salt water stones and two beautiful rocks. The first Nathan recognized as an aggregate of feldspar with pockets of quartz and garnet, the second a large "ball" of glistening quartz.

In a few minutes Vivian left and returned with three fresh baked warm partridgeberry muffins,

"…baked dese myself just before you came over. I really didn't know you'd be comin'."

Vivian handed one to Nathan who continued speaking with Jamie about the quartz.

He watched her eyes as she reached down to help her boy, but Jamie reached in to help himself, his mouth in no time smeared with berry juice.

She smiled, looking up and lingering for a moment on Nathan's eyes, her face and neck grew warm.

Vivian bit into her muffin. Tying Jamie's shoelace she again looked up at this young man, some years ago a classmate in school, and closely searched his face.

"Philip's mother is going to look after Jamie during de week," Vivian broke into the silence, "Naomi is sendin' me to school for the year in St. Anthony, to learn taking care of patients and learnin' computers."

Jamie suddenly tugged at Nathan's arm and impulsively blurted out whether he wanted to play soccer before supper? The ball still lay beside the path. It was kicked and the game began. Soon five other lads and two girls from the cove joined in. Rules were quickly made up and as quickly forgotten. Vivian had not seen, nor heard Jamie play for a long time.

An hour passed and the exhausted Nathan and young Jamie sat side by side on the back bridge of the clinic drinking hot chocolate.

~ ~

His parents, Dennis and Olivia, needed Nathan to stay home. His father's altered features told him so. Through the early months of the year, Olivia noticed Dennis' gradual weight loss and periods of painful coughing and shortness of breath. Dennis never spoke of it and, furthermore, could not be persuaded to see Naomi at the clinic.

Now with Nathan home, Dennis became somewhat more amenable and agreed that Naomi make her home visit.

This morning Dennis registered a fever. Naomi examined him and obtained several specimens of blood and urine, placed them into her refrigerated bag and carried them to the clinic for assessment. That evening she made the referral.

Following Nathan's strained homecoming last Christmas, and lately Dennis' general malaise, Olivia had rarely slept through the night. For the first time in her life, she had felt, at least momentarily, forsaken. Her son's passiveness towards the cruel attack against his beloved Jenny left Olivia burdened in soul and heartbroken. How does a young woman get filled with so much spite and hatred – perhaps because Jenny is filled with so much good, she thought.

Jenny had met Nathan in the early morning of his arrival. Naomi saw them standing together, speaking, walking together hand in hand along the landwash. Nathan did not come in for a long while, but when he did, it was with Jenny.

He greeted his mother with a kiss on the nape of her neck. Naomi had turned to the stove. No one had to tell her what very recently transpired between them. Tears of release and gratitude ran down her cheeks.

~ ~

Dennis consented to travel across the straits and up to St. Anthony for assessment. However, rather than being flown to hospital by the Grenfell air transport, he insisted that Nathan drive him down the coast in his own boat.

Late the following afternoon, while his father stayed over in hospital, Nathan loaded the bottom of his boat with boxes of groceries – eggs, milk, flour, grains and rice, frozen chicken pies, and a pound of frozen cod tongues. Before he left St. Anthony, he secured the boxes against the imminent change of weather on the open sea.

As many Newfoundlanders who live by the sea, Nathan had an innate sense of tomorrow's weather. He knew the sea off these northern shores intimately from years on the water with his father. In the open sea along these sculpted shores, he had also known fear.

Whereas the sea remained flat for their trip that morning, on this return, however, as he headed northwest and away from land, a strong cross-wind came up from the northeast. He could see from his starboard side white combers breaking over the shoals of Belle Isle in the distance. As he passed Quirpon Island, a pod of humpback whales surfaced to his left, two breached gracefully ahead of him, and then another, their flippers and flukes smacking the surface of the water. From his starboard side, rounding Cape Norman on his left, Nathan watched as the vast expanse of the Labrador Sea opened, as if in slow motion, restless and dark before him.

In a quarter hour waves began to menace the boat to drift astern. By his experienced handling from the rudder only a few swept over the gunnels.

With the wind came a light rain. Soon pelting rain struck his face and blinded his visibility. For the better part of an hour Nathan could not see ahead by even ten feet. Nevertheless, he knew that he knew his way home by gut-sense and instinct.

Nathan loved the movements of this boat that Dennis and he, as a boy of nine, had carved out near to ten years ago.

The rain abated unexpectedly, but not the wind. Rocked with the rhythm of the swells, Nathan felt a surge of triumph — he was master in his wooden craft, alone with the wind on the sea that he loved. In a few hours Nathan spotted the barren islands outlined between his boat and shore, silhouetted in the descending dusk.

Rounding one of the islands, he pulled aside a small growler and chopped off eight large chunks of glacial ice to keep in the freezer back home.

From the far side of the bay Olivia had watched the downpour from her front window. As it moved to the south and west, she spotted him first rising on a crest and then disappearing into its swell. Again she saw him rise. She clasped her hands and whispered a quiet thank you.

He navigated through the tickle that divided the larger island from the "Ilse a'Drift," as the locals nicknamed her, and felt a surge of pride — *yes, like his father*, she mused, *Nathan was born for the water.*

Olivia watched as he secured the boat against the pier and, as she had hoped, walk over to Jamie's wagon resting at the stage entrance. The boy had brought it down for Nathan to pull the groceries up the circuitous pathway to the house.

Before he entered through the back door, Nathan smelled the fresh, thick soup Olivia made that morning. She simmered it through the afternoon. It was the soup that greeted his father over the many years when he came home from hauling in his catch damp, stiff from the cold and hungry.

"How's Dad when you left 'im?"

"He doesn't like being away from home. Dr. Ferg'son examined him for quite a stretch, then left for a while to figure it all out, I guess. When he did return his recommendation was for Dad to stay a while… get checked out further. Dr. Ferg'son did find an infection somewhere inside Dad from the blood Naomi took off him. She had faxed the results. Oh yes, he said there was also low oxygen count in the blood." The nurse came in and started an intravenous drip a few minutes after that. She also placed a short oxygen tube to run into Dad's nose. He complained of shortness of breath on the way over and still had it. You know, he's always quiet about things so it must have bothered him some."

After a minute's silence, "Dennis can't see that he's getting' older. He cut and hauled dat wood earlier on in winter. Big Al came over to help pile it in full cords out back. A face cord dey left stacked beside the road, 'cause Dennis couldn't 'andle it all.

"Remember dat storm at Amanda and Philip's wedding when they secured dem dorries and t'ings? Well, his lower back inflamed over it, dey said, and near gave way. His pain was wonderful bad. Ian and Naomi X-rayed it and brought over a physiotherapist from St. Anthony. He's to sit up straight wid a pillow at his lower back. Mostly he doesn't – forgets 'e says."

"This morning as we got the boat ready for the crossing, Dad says – 'Can't leave Olivia for long, never forever if you know what I mean.'"

"Yes," Olivia slowly shook her head, becoming more thoughtful, "his nerves gets in de' blood so strong whenever he t'inks about dyin' and leavin' me and of course dis place he loves. Never lived outside de cove here, he hasn't."

Olivia continued, "Dat large patch of Labrador Tea flowers out back where 'tis a bit mossy, and with all dem shrubs... well he used to sit der under the black spruce, the ones next to the tamaracks," she pointed to the spot... "for hours, just 'tinkin, he says... an' I told him, age comes against us sooner or late and changes 'tings, and someday will end 'tings...and den He takes us to Hi'self."

Expected footfalls were heard running along the path. Seconds later they leaped up the stairs of the bridge and burst through the kitchen door and into the kitchen filled with the fragrance of fresh warm cinnamon-swirl bread and bakeapple muffins. It was Jamie.

Twenty minutes on, he and Nathan left with the wagon, a loaf of fresh and still-warm partridgeberry bread, and a dozen lingonberry muffins.

Amanda came to the clinic earlier that afternoon. She thought herself to be around eleven weeks pregnant.

"I'm checking in," she said as she greeted Naomi and Vivian.

"I noticed you sitting in the waiting area – your smile and dimples gave you away, and I am probably right guessing as to why."

"Yes, and I haven't told Philip yet, not before it's confirmed."

Following dinner, Vivian left the house a few minutes after Jamie ran off to pick up his wagon. Now she too ran, along the pathway. Amanda was sitting on the front bridge expecting her friend with two steaming mugs of bakeapple.

Philip came out the front door with a mug of coffee and greeted Vivian warmly. He stood quietly to the side peering out into the distance, a bit daunted, she thought, as if drinking his coffee was all he was able to handle after taking in Amanda's news.

Behind the cove and separating their small island from the mainland, a tickle flowed quite shallow at low tide. At high tide a small banking dory or rodney was required to pass over. At low tide a pickup could easily bridge the water.

A while after Nathan and Jamie delivered the wagon with its contents and for the hour waited awhile until the tickle lowered to knee-depth before driving the pickup across. Very soon the remaining firewood left standing by the gravel road was on its way over. The fellows unloaded the wood which when stacked, added up to more than a face cord, quite dry enough and sufficient for some weeks to ward off the autumn cold.

Vivian did not return home by way of the path. Rather she crossed the narrow "field of tuckamores," a cluster of low-growth pines common to the coast. Coming up to the rear of the house she spotted the neatly piled firewood and suspected Nathan. It had to be him. It was. He and Jamie were sitting together midst the cut wood around them, both filling up with a slice of fresh bread layered with berry jam.

Vivian walked towards them, her eyes never leaving Nathan's. She checked herself, yet wanted desperately to snuggle against him.

As she had just confided in Amanda, "to feel 'im, 'is arms round me 'nd never stop kissing me... dat's how I finally got to sleep, feelin' 'im, smelling 'im, kissin' 'im..."

Jamie ran up to her gulping down the last mouthful, talking excitedly, telling her about the wood and how they had crossed over the tickle in a truck, about the three moose they had seen grazing along the road, about the bear on the far side of the lake, and the RCMP car driving past them towards Mary's Harbour...

"...it's a surprise for you, Mom," Jamie burst out.

She reached down to hug her son, "T'ank you," she looked again at Nathan, "both of you."

"We brought some muffins and stuff for you too; dey're from Nathan's mom...

"We ate a couple just before you came," he added a bit more slowly and sheepishly.

Nathan had not yet spoken a word but continued to look at Vivian. *"She is so beautiful, her face, her lips, the way she speaks, her voice, her form... all of her..."* he thought to himself, afraid that she might see. She did see.

Later in the evening, Vivian and Nathan talked for hours. Jamie claimed to be completing his homework, yet he listened intently, and watched as Nathan and his mother edged closer to each other. Jamie feigned sleep when Vivian came to kiss him good night and tuck him in.

As she turned towards the door, and believing him to be asleep, he spoke, "are you two 'n item?"

Vivian turned and walked back to him, "I don't know... I 'ope so."

"Me too. I really like him. Where's he now?"

"Nathan's gone 'ome. Tomorrow de Grenfell 's flying his father home from hospital and he'll spend 'a few days wid us 'n de clinic."

"Is he very sick?"

"Yes but 'everyone t'inks 'e'll be 'ok."

She tussled his hair, kissed him again, turned and walked to the door. Just before she closed it behind her, she added, "'e likes you lots too."

Jamie smiled broadly and nodded his head in agreement.

Vivian went into work for ten-thirty the following morning. Before that she met Amanda in the small café next to the church. They drank their coffee and ate croissants, talked cheerfully and shared the very recent "cove gossip" – as Philip called it – until the time came for Vivian to go.

Close to noon hour, an RCMP cruiser that had crossed the tickle at low tide drove up to the clinic. The lady officer asked for Vivian, to speak with her alone.

Vivian led her to the side room. After they were seated, the officer began her questions.

"Please take your time to answer," she spoke softly. "Do you know David Lapierre?"

Vivian became troubled. She nodded, "yes."

"When did you see him last?"

"A year and five months, I t'ink. David was working seasonally 'n Toronto, 'n 'after dat he moved to Calgary… wid somebody else."

There was a pause. The officer waited for Vivian to continue. She became aware of her hands shaking. With her voice quivering Vivian continued. "I've kept his note… says 'e found someone else, an' never loved me."

"You have a child with him?"

Vivian became mortified thinking ahead, *maybe David wants Jamie for hi'self.* Her eyes filled with tears. "Yes… Jamie."

"How old is Jamie?"

"He turned nine 'n May." Vivian raised her eyebrows.

"I'm sorry. Please this has nothing directly to do with Jamie. I must inform you that David died early yesterday in a motor vehicle accident. He was still alive when they placed him on the stretcher. That is when he whispered both your names and that you lived here. That is all he could say."

"'ow did 't happen?"

"He had been drinking. It began as a row in the bar and that led to a fight. David left in his car. Witnesses testified that he was quite intoxicated. On his way home, he was speeding when the car hit the soft shoulders, then a tree and spun into a ravine. The impact threw David about a hundred feet. He was alone."

Vivian sat without speaking for what seemed many minutes. *"What is there to say,"* she thought. Her fingers dug into the flesh of her left arm. The upsurge of shame and grief for having been discarded began as an excruciating compressing pain in her chest. She bowed her head as if hiding from the kindly officer sitting beside her.

"No one came in to claim his body, so unless you wish otherwise, he will be buried by the city. There will be a clergyperson."

Vivian heard nothing. The officer left.

Naomi called Amanda who came immediately. She held Vivian in her arms gently stroking her hair.

~ ~

Nathan's license to cut for firewood allotted him the same plot given last year to Dennis. It remained a parcel of land resource rich in trees. Regardless of the gneiss and limestone bedrock, seedlings had sprouted throughout any open areas available to them. Therefore, to cut here for another year would not leave the land liable to defoliation and barrenness. Nathan's father had an ingrained sense of conservation that Nathan himself had inculcated since boyhood. This included hunting and fishing as much as respecting the forest and the minutiae of flowers.

For a long while he sat on a log, not a scrap of thought considering those values passed on, but reliving his time with Vivian over and over. Her freckles, her kisses and softness as she leaned into him, and her eyes – they held him spellbound.

Nathan sat oblivious to all else, lulled away from the wood and the moose again grazing nearby, by feelings, by a passion he had never before known with anyone. He and Vivian lived in this cove their entire lives. For most of those years, they lived only five houses apart, went to the same schools on the mainland, their fathers fished together and their mothers tended to both children and encouraged them to read.

Nathan knew David almost as long. As a child folks described him as likeable yet quite a ticket. At school his brief attention span made him restless. When David came to adolescence the family moved to New Brunswick, "where the family's from," David had told Vivian.

David came back to the cove a year later, presumably, he said, to court Vivian.

"I couldn't live without you with me," David told her one night.

When Vivian became pregnant David began his longer absences from home. He found work in Toronto and came home for a visit, but not until Jamie's first birthday.

During these brief homecomings, usually twice a year, he doted on Jamie, his son, and the boy clung to his father. As Jamie became older he began to sense his father's desire to move on, "back to where the work is good... so I can send you and mommy more money to eat and go to school."

To Vivian, the two weeks David was home, he remained the ardent lover, father and husband. She took the time he gave her gratefully and through the years never suspected anything amiss.

Abruptly, within the month before Christmas, the money stopped coming. Then in spring came the note declaring David's intensions to move further west.

Nathan came to know all this. While at university last year his mother wrote and mentioned David's abandonment,

"...and, in truth, betrayal. Vivian has been devastated. Apparently she feels so worthless she now feels... and trying to explain some of this to Jamie, Vivian told us near Christmas, 't'was like clubbing to dea't a newly barn'd fawn.'"

Still sitting on the log next to his chain saw, Nathan reached into his backpack and began eating lunch. There were several tuna fish sandwiches Olivia made from the boatload of groceries he had brought across yesterday, and a thermos of her favourite tea. He never drank tea but for this morning there was nothing else except water from the brook that trickled past him.

Later Nathan strode along its bank and down to the lake with his fishing rod. It was a lake the locals knew as teeming with abundant fresh water fish. Two or three minutes after Nathan's fishing line and hook hit the cold Labrador water, he pulled in a sizeable lake trout. In another twenty minutes, he had two larger trout and three land-locked salmon.

This was enough for today. He had fished for himself and Olivia, and for Vivian. There was sufficient bounty in that lake for tomorrow.

At that, he packed up. Because of high tide, Nathan left the truck and crossed the tickle in his canoe stored on shore opposite the cove side.

He had as yet no idea as to what had surfaced this morning. For all Nathan knew, Vivian began work in the clinic by mid morning. So with the tackle and chainsaw left in the truck, Nathan paddled over the tickle with the fish and headed home to clean and fillet them. Being skilled and having worked on the water for years, the fish were cleaned quickly before Olivia even noticed him home.

"Dere's been de police over de clinic dis morning... come to see Vivian I 'ear."

Nathan handed her the fish. "What's it about?" Worried now, he tried to think. "Is she, Vivian I mean, okay?"

"Don't rightly know m'son, 'cept she's just gone 'ome, 'and de RCMP lady went back cross to de mainland."

Nathan walked down to his father's stage. Something in Olivia's voice about not knowing, but she did say that the police had come across the tickle and met with Vivian. He busied himself. The boat needed baling from water having come over the gunnels during yesterday's crossing.

"This 's how 'e reacts when unsure of his'elf," Olivia spoke aloud watching Nathan walking down to the landwash.

She also saw Jamie. He sat on "Nathan's rock," a special place where Nathan always sat since childhood, whenever "I have hard thinking to do," he had said.

He came over the rocks to where Jamie sat. "That used to be my favourite place to sit."

The boy looked up for only a moment. To Nathan the boy looked angry or confused – perhaps both. Nathan sat down on a nearby piece of driftwood. There was a long silence.

"Why didn't my Dad stay here with us? Now 'es dead an' he ain't never comin' back. Mom keeps saying to Naomi that 'e got tired of us hangin' round his neck."

" ... and you were waiting for him to come home this year."

Jamie shook his head, "yeah... but 'e didn't... Mom said that 'e was speeding and went off de road. Dat's what killed 'im. It was an accident...I miss 'im... he used to take me out 'n de boat... Mom packed a picnic and der's our favourite spot out der on de island..."

Jamie looked down and wiped his nose with the back of his hand. Tears ran down his face. His shoulders shook. Nathan came over to sit beside him. The boy moved towards him. Nathan placed his arm around his shoulders. Soon Jamie leaned into him, crying.

Vivian had come down to the landwash. She stood very still, watching them, listening.

After a few minutes Nathan looked towards the wharf. Their eyes met and both knew what neither had yet spoken...

Jamie turned, his face flushed and his eyes swollen.

"De boys," as she later called them, stood up and walked up to her.

"We've got some fresh fish for dinner, if you want. I brought in from the lake today. Mom said for me to ask you both over. She's got two coffee cakes packed full with blueberries in the oven."

Turning towards Jamie, "No ice cream though."

"Yes Nathan, dat'll be lovely. T'ank you."

Together they walked slowly up from the wharf.

Nathan turned his head and looked past Jamie, "I love you," he whispered, barely audible.

Stunned, Vivian read him and understood but could not answer. No parent or lover ever confessed such feelings to her, or spoke back her love for them.

Amanda, her friend, loved her. Jamie loved her. Vivian knew it and returned their loves unconditionally.

"But this," she told Jamie at bedtime, "feels like standing 'on de shore, 'in de waves 'an de pebbles moving beneath my feet."

V

Iceberg Near St. Anthony

Laura had flown to St. Anthony to be with Cynthia. She really did not know her well. To Cynthia, Laura's presence was, nevertheless, comforting and familiar. They had met a few times in Kingston, most often during the months of Llewellan's illness.

By the time Ron was taken from the sailboat to the nursing station on the island he had already lost a significant amount of blood. Naomi presumed into the large intestine. When Ron arrived in casualty his blood pressure dropped precipitously. He did not recognize Cynthia. Once in hospital immediate examination revealed a life-threatening bowel obstruction and rupture that required critical surgery.

Four hours later Ron was wheeled into ICU for post-op recovery. Here he was expected to remain for the next several days.

Three days after Laura arrived, she and Isabelle met for lunch at Fishing Point, a restaurant that was once home to the lighthouse keeper and his family. Laura arrived early and spent the time looking out over the North Atlantic. A refreshing sun shower fell as a light mist. Turning to face south she looked up at the massive granite cliffs, rock walls rising straight up out of the water. By the passing of eons and the unrelenting beating of wind and sea their base had become worn and smooth. She heard the cry of seagulls swooping down and around a small fishing boat. The vessel appeared so diminutive set against the cliffs above it. She could scarcely make out the lone fisherman standing at her stern.

Isabelle saw Laura leaning up against a large rock, a lonely figure. Laura saw only the sea and the sun rising and the mist dispelling in its wake. Lost in thought Laura could feel her life taking a very different turn. She stood there struggling to understand.

Hearing someone's footsteps on the loose rocks behind her Laura turned. She smiled before Isabelle was even aware she had been noticed. The beauty of the sea, the sound of the surf and the mantle of flowers, berries and foliage beside the paths always held her spellbound, hearing and seeing these things as if it were for the first time.

Laura sat down on a bench. Isabelle followed. Both looked out to sea and saw a pod of three or four humpback whales swimming north lunge feeding as they passed.

Neither had yet spoken.

"It was so good of you to come for Susan's wedding," Isabelle broke the silence, "She was very glad to see you."

"Yes, I'm glad to have come. I didn't know how she would take me coming after all the grief and tension I caused."

"What I do know is that Susan was very grateful to have had you there."

"I almost didn't you know. That is now, what, you know, ah… really scares me. Looking back only a few days, it hasn't sunk in yet… this is my only daughter getting married…" Laura looked away and sat silently for a few minutes. She turned to Isabelle. Her eyes were red. Tears ran down the sides of her nose and over her cheek. She wiped them, slowly, "and Susan would have been haunted by the knowledge had I not come. I would have left a void in her memory of this day… and the accusations I threw her way. I am her mother. For me it might have been a desperate regret."

In spite of what she just said, by now Laura had become aware of a recurring, disquieting ambivalence, and again that feeling of an imposing unreality, *where I feel almost cut off from what I'm saying,* she thought. Nevertheless, she continued.

"A friend came around and stood up to me, early morning two days before the wedding… he helped me to realize how blind I had become, so wrapped up in my own anger and disappointment… It hit me like a rock, a shock… I began to shake… I could have easily cut myself off from her forever… then I almost panicked, dreading, hoping, praying not to be late. He dropped by later to help me get the trip together."

"Where had all this come from, do you know?"

"I think so… ah, a little bit anyway. When Richard died that morning I thought everything would be okay. There is still Susan. I have Susan."

"But it wasn't, okay I mean?"

"No." Laura shook her head, then continued.

"When I missed Susan's plane, I feared that perhaps she wasn't coming. I began to feel abandoned and, ah… terrified… and when she did arrive, I was angry and frustrated. That first day she was home I felt like screaming 'don't you understand…you are rejecting me…stay home with me…' and when she left again, I unglued, as it were, and said awful things to her that no mother should ever even think…

"…but gradually over these past years I knew it wasn't really Susan. It all stems from way back when my mother left the five of us…"

Laura stopped in mid-sentence. She watched as the whales swam towards a foreland, rounded it and disappeared.

Laura reached into her purse and pulled out a small leather box, opened it and showed Isabelle the silver pocket watch Richard had treasured and carried for years."

His uncle gave it to Richard, then still a young man, the very evening he died.

"Richard never parted from this watch except in his final days. After that it has always been in here. The few times it wasn't, I had misplaced it. I became frantic, desperate to find it... somehow it linked us together... I mean Richard is here with me again. The watch recalls how close we were together." Laura paused, "but then it was not always like that. We did love each other, but there were many times...," she paused again.

"There were long tense silences between us... sometimes a week went by when neither of us spoke to the other. We would undress for bedtime alone somewhere so the other wouldn't see. We openly fought over Susan... she needed her own life but I resisted. Richard understood her.

"Over these last five years I have had to struggle to let go the pocket watch and release those links. I still can't do it."

Laura again paused, looked away to the lighthouse, "and now, Isabelle, I wonder, if I purchased some appropriate clothes, I might remain here for the week Susan will be gone... There wasn't time for us to talk and I just want to know my child again... I've missed all these years... and ask her to forgive me. What will Susan be doing once she returns?"

"I don't know. Susan is returning for a few more weeks on Friday. However following this, they are both leaving for her university course, and Martin's helicopter rescue training out west. The Grenfell has hired both when they return in two years. Just a month ago Susan bought a house in Ship Cove, just north of here."

Laura stood up, her mouth open, her eyes wide, her hands trembling. She did not speak.

She leaned against Isabelle.

"Now, I know this Lighthouse Restaurant up ahead has the best fish cakes and chowder on the Island. Let's go for lunch."

They sat by the windows overlooking the red and white lighthouse.

"This is one of many around the coast of Newfoundland and Labrador," Isabelle recounted. "These lighthouses are often called our "coastal guardians" and have saved the lives of countless seamen and crew, and at the helm of every lighthouse were men and families willing to sacrifice their own safety, even their lives. These families braved incredible winds, snow and ice to save those on floundering ships, crashing against menacing cliffs and jagged sunkers, lost in fog, men and women hurled violently into the frigid sea."

Laura sat in a distracted silence.

Isabelle continued by relating several such past crises on Belle Isle, a large barren island sitting just north eastward from Fishing Point.

The warmed berry pie ended the meal.

"You and Susan are very close friends," Laura asked falteringly, fearing the answer.

"Yes." Isabelle read Laura's suspicion.

Laura's questioning became abrupt. She asked about Wilfred Grenfell, "that missionary physician who has left such a lasting influence on Susan, and now you Isabelle. I'm quite amazed at that, but I'm trying to see what Susan sees, what you see...

"Why really did you decide to come here, Isabelle, and stay after you finished those six months? What keeps you here?"

"I live in town, as you know, away from the actual hospital. The people from the coves and the bays, here and up the coasts are so incredibly different from anywhere I have ever lived.

"Yes, there is grief and tragedy, people die, some at sea, others succumb to the cold on land, others at home, a very few by their own hand. They have their loves and some their hates. Occasionally someone's inebriated behaviour and abuse causes terrible hardship. Where doesn't it?

"The town's folk took me in and offered to teach me how to bake my own bread and cook a moose dinner for some of my friends at the hospital."

As a people, Newfoundlanders are over-comers, having been bullied by foreign interests, and at times by their own government. They remain a people who support one another. Newfoundlanders have strong family ties and generally they live unencumbered by the noises of the city and, I might add, I never lock my doors at night, or while at work.

"I love the people here whether as friends, neighbours or patients. I have made some wonderful friends here and along the coast – and I love the stillness.

"The last week before the wedding Susan asked me to come up to Nain. One afternoon I hiked north to Conche Bay where Susan and I love to spend some of our off days, just to read, to talk or merely to sit on a cliff high above the Labrador Sea and listen to the silence, or to hear the movement of the sea by the shore or, occasionally to watch a herd of caribou, or even a lone wolf. I've tried to describe what it is like for me to sit there – finally I have no description; it just is! And that is why I am here and not there, back in the city. Quite simply, here I have come home.

"I have come to love Amanda and Philip Patey dearly. Actually you met him some years back in Kingston. They both returned to the coast after their respective graduate programs at Queen's University. She told me that they both fell in love at a Bach concert."

Not hearing, Laura had drifted into her very private, absorbed silence. Isabelle felt her withdrawal.

Laura did not stay the week. For her this was not home, nor did it compare with sights and sounds with which she was familiar. Following her lunch with Isabelle, Laura returned to her Bed and Breakfast. She lay down for a nap but lay awake restless. With mounting tension, she rose and went outside shivering against the cool evening air.

"I'm so bored," Laura whispered to herself. "and now I'm cold," as she wrapped her sweater up around her neck.

"I'm so angry at Susan," she spoke out sharply, "even Isabelle speaks as out of a dream world. No, I won't put up with it, and I will not apologize to Susan. Why must I? Why, really, am I in this forgotten place?"

Laura did not sleep all night. As the long night hours trudged on, she became increasingly angry. Time ticked away interminably. In the early morning she skipped breakfast, left a note to cancel the two weeks already reserved, and another at the hospital switchboard for Isabelle to pass on to Susan.

She then promptly telephoned a taxi for the airport. Laura found herself on standby. She waited two hours. The first snow began to fall.

"It's only September," she whispered to herself. "Incredible!"

Because of last minute booking Laura's flight to Ottawa became a circuitous aggravation. She left St. Anthony at ten in the morning and finally arrived home after a protracted and unexpected stopover in St. John's.

Once outside the late afternoon air felt unusually humid for the season. Laura was driven home from the airport through the scrambled, yet everyday noise of traffic.

Leaving an armful of groceries on the kitchen counter, Laura sank into her familiar sofa, a fresh cup of coffee steaming in her hand, the hush in the room broken only by the ongoing ticking of the clock.

In the ticking, she recalled her last chat with Susan, centuries ago in the past it seemed, yet in this very room. Glancing towards the clock, Laura suddenly remembered that Susan would be arriving in St. Anthony, Friday, in this very hour. She stared across the room and sat in tense solitude, brooding in the silence.

"Susan has been headstrong… yes, she has offended me deeply by actually going through with the wedding to this man, in that uncultivated place, away from everything we have given her… Yes, she alone is to blame… she cut herself off… Why?…" Laura spoke as if in a groan, grimaced and began to tremble, spilling her coffee over the arm of the sofa.

"What a self-willed, contrary, ungrateful child we raise… and how did I ever buy into actually going there?

"By doing so Susan probably read my approval into it. Well, I don't approve, and neither does your father," Laura screamed at the chair Susan had sat in the night after the funeral, revealing that she loved this man.

"He's a pilot, she claimed, just to defend herself." Laura paused from her monologue. "Yes, it was guilt that drove me to go, wasn't it, but I have no guilt," she whispered to herself. Her teeth clenched in rage.

A silence and the ticking filled the drawing room.

Laura began to cry and forgot the spill and the soiling stain scarring her new sofa. Shaking and sobbing – she just didn't know why. She held her hands over her face as if to shield herself from anyone seeing.

There was no one.

~ ~

On the return flight east Susan sat by the window. As the Island came into view, the pilot began his calibrated descent, soon allowing Susan to focus on the land, its fjords, hills and inlets, lakes and waterfalls created and scoured by ancient glacial ice.

It is all so beautiful, like nowhere else, she thought.

The plane banked starboard. She peered down into the pine forests of Gros Morne and the highway that would begin taking them north along the Gulf of St. Lawrence.

Philip met them in St. Anthony and all three drove at once to the Lighthouse Restaurant for dinner. There they met Isabelle appearing wrapped in thought while looking out to sea. She usually relished her scones and tea but today they were left untouched.

Her friends came through the red door entrance and before their presence registered Susan had run up to her. After an initial spirited embrace, Isabelle's favourite table by the window became full of animated chatter.

Susan noticed her cold tea and pastry, and picked up that Isabelle's attention slipped slowly away from the group. Susan knew that it did not have anything to do with a difficult surgical case Isabelle had finished just prior to coming.

The dinner was delicious. When it came time for dessert, Susan and Isabelle went outside. Walking to the Lighthouse at the Point, they each sat on the rounded bench.

Isabelle sat silently for a minute. Susan reached across and held her hand.

"Your mother left here in quite a state. Laura intended to wait for you and Martin. We had, at least what I thought to be a terrific chat, she and I, right here, sitting on those flat rocks next to you. We then went in to eat and continued to chat. A few hours later I was on call and so left her at the Bed and Breakfast.

"In the morning the hostess telephoned the hospital saying that Laura had left early for the airport, 'somewhat agitated,' she recounted. "Laura left a note for me to eventually pass on to you."

Isabelle reached for the folded note and gave it to Susan who had already sensed its acrimonious and berating content. A short ways into the letter her hands shook.

> *To our daughter Susan:*
>
> *...I've had time to think about everything that has happened these few days. When I arrived for the wedding, even already in Gander, things came at me too quickly and I had no time to get accustomed to things up there. You were a very inconsiderate daughter not to have waited at least for a few days following my*

arrival before you went forward with that unruly wedding, and to that strange man who will never appreciate you and because of his own selfish ends will use you… and who has ever heard of a Moravian minister, and an Eskimo at that, no one. Your friend Isabelle, I had lunch with her… she is, what can I say, out of it, so to speak, unrealistic, a romantic. She even made me question myself. Consequently, I have lost you as long as you persist in dashing our hopes for you. On your way out west I will appreciate it if you do not visit me with that man…

Susan read no further. "Let's not tell anyone about this letter."

"I'm so sorry, Susan. I almost didn't give it to you."

Martin and Philip finished their warmed partridgeberry pie, came out and walked over to the bench. By then Susan's eyes were red, her handkerchief soggy with irrepressible tears shed over a most cruel judgement and the sting of injustice – and this not from a stranger, rather from her mother who had once nursed and cradled her, who has now brought herself to within a stone's throw of disowning her.

Martin did pick up the letter as it lay on the bench. He read Laura's berating message through to its finish, said nothing to anyone and walked slowly back to the car. Returning to the bench, he brought a blanket and wrapped it around Susan…

~ ~

The ensuing two years brought with them significant changes. Martin and Susan settled into their graduate residence in Vancouver. At the end of those years, she had earned her Masters Degree in health sciences and certification as a Nurse Practitioner. Martin completed the requisite training year to become licensed as a helicopter pilot. Both left the west coast to begin work out of the St. Anthony hospital; he as a pilot, Susan to set up a wound clinic. The following week they both moved to Ship Cove, north of St. Anthony, into a renovated house they had purchased while home the year before.

Vivian commuted from the island to St. Anthony on weekdays for most of the following eighteen months while Nathan filled their freezers with fish and game, and cut seven full cubic cords of firewood for both houses. He and Jamie became inseparable.

Jamie had struggled in school until well after Christmas the year his father died.

~ ~

During Vivian's time at the hospital she was given a placement in the Intensive Care unit. One mid-afternoon a man was brought up from Emergency, having been discovered slumped over in his car and unconscious.

Although Vivian had not seen him, or his family in many years, she did recognize him. Clive Thompson, she was once told, had "disappeared" into western Canada leaving his wife and family behind, some saying that the marriage was strained, others claiming that he had to leave the Island for work.

Years before in '92, following the Moratorium, life had been stressful for Clive and the family. The government orders for quotas of fish could never support a young family of six. A quiet, kind yet private man, he never spoke much. With the loss of both the cod, and the money to clothe and feed the children, came the profound loss of who he knew himself to be.

As long as physically able and as soon as the ice moved out of the harbour, he had lived, like many another, as a fisherman's son, born for the sea and the fishery, and never dreamed of doing anything else. From his earliest years as a boy in the cove, Clive was on the water. No government compensation today could heal the moratorium wounding, nor in any way make up for the feeling of casting out your nets in the morning, bringing them back up packed with fish, then proudly walking home for dinner.

Nevertheless, today Clive neared exhaustion as he drove the long road north alongside the straits. Veering east, Clive hoped to be able to make St. Anthony. Clive had always enjoyed this six hour trip with the sea to port and, for some distance, the Long Range Mountains rising to starboard. Yet not today. He felt very sick.

In the past he fondly remembered that along this Range the northern winter transforms the land of stacked lobster traps, tuckamore, even the bogs into expanses of glistening silver bathed by the radiance of the noon sun. In another setting, however, this marvel was deceptive. Like the ice to his left, it could change in an instant by the wind and current.

Each time he drove this road, Clive relived one of his past trips north from Deer Lake. Past Flowers Cove, and an hour from St. Anthony, a snow-drenched, screeching sea wind from over the water buried his car within the next several miles. Ahead of the burial he had watched the steep snow banks on the west side collapsing over the road ahead of him.

Having tied a rope from the steering shaft, he crawled out and walked around the car all night.

After the storm settled, Clive listened intently for the sound of any distant engine. No one knew that he was there and all he heard were the ice crystals drifting and tinkling across the frozen snow. It was not until the following afternoon that he did hear, at first very faintly, the engines of two snowplows, one coming, as yet unseen, towards him from the south, another like a speck akin to a vanishing point from the north. The drivers spotted him on top of the snow – Clive had walked round and round his car since late yesterday morning, crawling down into the car several times to drink hot tea from a thermos. He had heard of many a man and woman dying out here, one just the other night, needlessly and alone, in their car, the man's hands grasped around an emptied and lethal flask of whiskey.

Some years following the Moratorium, Clive had left home, his wife Dea and the four children, Imogen being the eldest, fully resolved to find work on the mainland, perhaps Ontario. Ever since the Cod Moratorium, things had not come together for the family, and tensions grated.

His intention was to stay for the remainder of that year. He remained for two, then three. Three became ten. Eventually, Clive found construction work farther west in Victoria.

Somewhere in these years, he heard talk that Dea "found" another man from up the shore a short ways, and the children seemed quite happy and settled. From then on Clive no longer sent Dea the bulk of his monthly earnings. For the past years it was sent regularly, yet without much notice from the family – now everything stopped. No one so much as commented.

All of Clive's other letters to Dea remained unopened – yet none of them were returned. From the first year of his absence, no one in the family ever expressed a word of bitterness or sense of loss – Clive had become no longer relevant. Life just went on and on without him. This was noticeably real following the arrival of Nelson, the other man and "my greatest love ever," as Dea was wont to say.

Last May, a team of doctors in Victoria diagnosed Clive as having a malignant growth that had spread menacingly into his spine and lungs.

He felt ill and weakened for some months, even as far back as last December. Occasionally he coughed up blood-streaked sputum. Nevertheless, Clive held it off until he barely had strength to last a half day's work and slept through every weekend. It was only when the couple living next door encouraged him to see their own physician that Clive's journey through a complete evaluation began. When it finished he heard the proposed trajectory of his now advanced illness.

His only thought was to return home to Newfoundland and the land for which he yearned, achingly. Furthermore, the thought of what awaited him there – what about Dea and his children, the other man – what about all these years? Fear and indecision borne of ambivalence tormented him during the long and quiet hours of most sleepless nights.

Following the definitive diagnosis, however, resolution and grit became stronger than fear. For two weeks he drove across Canada from the west coast to the east, resting more and more the closer he came. As Clive drove over the final rise, he saw St. Anthony, now so close.

He clutched the steering to control his tremors. Perspiration had soaked through his shirt. He felt nauseous, *"...as long as it just sits there,"* he thought. Putting it down to "nerves," Clive drove down the main street and past the Curtis Memorial Hospital. *"Hadn't it been called the Grenfell before I left?"*

It suddenly sounded so foreign, and the uncertain thought came to him –

"Where am I to go? I have nowhere!"

Fatigue, and a gripping sense of "lostness" overtook him. He began to cry as he drove to the end of the land, up to Fisherman's Point, and stopped the car. The lighthouse now beside him, the glacially frozen hills above him, the miles of sea ice ahead and below him all appeared unfocussed as if in a dense fog. Clive rubbed his face as if to clear his head,

"...yet it... O God..." his thoughts drifted off. He lost consciousness, his engine still running.

When Clive began to regain consciousness, he felt as if he was floating somewhere above it all, at first not at all comprehending anything around him, remembering only vaguely the Lighthouse. He envisioned seeing a dory moving out beyond the frozen bay.

"Now there were bottles," he thought, rising above his head and tubes in his arms. A form beside his bed stood up and came near. It was a girl he did not recognize. He tried to say something, and then fell back into a muddled sleep.

Isabelle and her staff were already aware of Clive's diagnosis. His regimen of medication, and the clinical notes dictated in Victoria were found, crinkled and stained among his belongings. It must have been an exceedingly difficult journey for Clive, a man so resolute to come home, and a man who arrived home just at the moment where he had no strength left to go further.

The hospital had searched for his next of kin but, for all anyone knew at the time of admission, they all lived off the Island and far into the central mainland – and that was about four years ago. That is, all but one.

Imogen had returned and was taking the computer and practical nursing course operated through the hospital, here in St. Anthony. She was now nineteen.

It was during the first days of her practical nursing course that Imogen met Vivian from the small island off southeast Labrador, and "we became buddies," as Vivian was to say more than once. Actually, each fondly remembered being playmates as children from two nearby coves. Both sat by the bed on this new morning after Clive's admission.

Imogen, there since early morning, became the form of someone her father sensed moving between consciousness and sleep. While Vivian left for morning class, Imogen continued her vigil beside her sleeping father. By noon Clive stirred and awakened. He had done so briefly a number of times since early morning.

His awareness still unfocussed and clouded, he tried to recognize the form now speaking to him. He knew that someone's hand stroked his forehead – fingers ran through his hair, gently and caressingly. A voice softly speaking to him aroused him to search through his haze to that someone. As if from a far off distance he began to know that voice. His hand slowly and weakly reached for the fingers of the hand that caressed him. The form continued to speak to him.

His eyes brightened, even just for a moment. His eyes closed. The form held his hand tighter now. In his thoughts he reached out to know her, and she came to him, and he began to cry as he drew closer to know her. Suddenly he did recognize and remember – she too was crying as she leaned forward. Imogen now held him and he knew it was she.

Vivian was given Imogen's father as her patient in ICU, to remain with him for bedside care and close monitoring. Clive was asleep.

"He knows me now," said Imogen as her friend entered, tears still running down her cheeks, "but his breathing has become a bit laboured, despite the oxygen. I think Dad is very critical."

Isabelle called in the surgeon. Dr. Stott came in shortly after, spent a long time examining Clive, and a longer time at the nursing station on the phone and reading the clinical notes Clive had brought with him. He gave new orders and spoke briefly to Isabelle before she entered the room. The nurse brought in the newly ordered medication to ease Clive's breathing. This she immediately injected into the drip.

"The protracted effort expended in coming home has claimed your father's strength, especially given his underlying illness. I think it time to phone your mother, or anyone else you feel should know." Isabelle spoke to Imogen softly but firmly.

Imogen sat beside her father, stroking his hand, tears again welling up. She listened to Isabelle, but didn't really hear her words. She watched her father and was grateful for their momentary recognition a while back, yet only now noticing the slight bluish tinge in his nail-beds and lips. His hands felt cold. His breathing became more and more irregular. She understood.

Day past into night. Imogen looked back over the last decade, even some years before, and became angry: "It was the waste and the unfairness. In the end we all just passed him off, yet over the years it could have been so much better. Dad meant well but Mother just dropped him. He had no one. If he still had us, Dad wouldn't be in this state."

Vivian sat beside her friend, listening, silently loving her, and Imogen knew it, gently squeezed her hand, and bowed her head. While in this dark chasm she prayed and pleaded for forgiveness: "So much waste, so much hurt and injustice cannot be covered by anything I can do, or even say," she whispered to God, "please, please take my father to Yourself."

Clive struggled with his laboured breathing through most of that night, yet he died peaceably in the early morning, Imogen holding his hand.

~ ~

DIARY: February 28

Dad's funeral was yesterday, the third sunrise of his passing. For two days I sent a fax, several e-mails and telephoned four times. I also left voice messages, but Mother did not answer. Nor did anyone. So, I was expecting to be alone with Dad. As it turned out Vivian remained with me day and night since Dad's death, and Amy came the day before the Service and stayed with us. Father Walters came; he officiated at the funeral. He has been so genuine and comforting to me through these last few difficult days.

A kindly old fisherman, Joe, and his wife Deloris from Goose Cove, offered to prepare Dad's body for burial. They have done this for the fishing families in the Cove and around so many times across the years. Deloris loaned me her own petite black veil for the mourning, a veil she herself had worn for her two young boys lost at sea some years back.

I only requested a few hours wake at the church on the morning of the funeral, because I thought no one would come. However, as Vivian, Amy and I went in together dozens of people from Goose Cove, my classmates and teachers from the hospital had gathered there. Several bouquets were placed around the coffin, and my own wreath on top. As it is a custom by many to lay a Crucifix on the deceased's chest, someone had done this for Dad. Father Walters met with us and we stood in a circle, all four of us, for prayer before we processed into the sanctuary.

He slowly spoke the ancient lines of liturgy and read from the Bible, and I will remember how his face seemed to light up and his deep voice rose with conviction. With the words, "...

and committing our brother Clive Thompson to Thy gracious keeping...," my eyes closed and my shoulders began to convulse. I must have felt the sudden impact of my grief with much the same words that I prayed when Dad began breathing his very last. I felt again the deep sadness of those lost years without him, and my Dad's final, lonely trip to desperately reach someone. In the end he did find that "someone," the person who really loved him — me.

Hands came onto my lap and circled each of mine. Following the Service the ladies of the Cove invited us all into the church hall. They had prepared a Newfoundlander's banquet, and to my surprise I was famished.

Tonight as I write this entry I feel sad but very blessed.

Imogen

~ ~

February was very cold. Fred sat by the newly stoked fire, bundled up in a dark green polyester shawl Judith had brought back from her last trip to St. John's in April. She was gone now, so every morning, like today, he sat alone in the stillness of the house, drinking a fresh mug of black coffee. He did so every evening as well.

Alone in these evenings Fred could almost feel her moving about in the kitchen or rustling about cleaning every corner. Today was Saturday and he smelled those berry-filled muffins that Judith always made on weekends. The kitchen was once so alight with her presence.

This morning no one was there.

In his chest he suddenly felt surges of aching loneliness. At times tears filled his eyes, yet he never made a sound.

Outside the wind screeching from the northeast dipped the thermometer to minus thirty-five. Last evening he remembered to ax a hole in the small waterfall and creek out back to bring in three large buckets of fresh drinking water, an extra one just in case.

In the early morning the entrance door facing the bay would have been frozen shut but for the deep drifts of snow that had overnight insulated the bayside of the cabin. The flames from the old stove crackled. His mug had become empty. He rose to fill it afresh from the Kerig, thankful that the storm had not yet pulled out the electricity.

Being the weekend Fred thought that perhaps Judith might come around – but he knew she hadn't called and it was too cold. "Even the snow plough hadn't begun to move any of it. No use doing that 'till nightfall anyway," he whispered.

His three children, grown now, had moved out some two years ago, a daughter Amy to Cape Breton, Timothy and Brent to Sault Ste. Marie in northeastern Ontario. Both boys have been working out on the Great Lakes.

Fred was often accused of being too hard on the boys. Tim, the youngest and the more sensitive, felt it more than Brent.

Most summers the boys fished inshore and cut firewood with their father. Tim was eleven the time he cut his finger on a knife blade while cleaning the family's quota of cod. The small cut became a rising in a few more hours. By later afternoon the boy's whole hand had swelled, but Fred refused to see it for what it was. Tim stayed with his father, trembling, and seemed to have developed a fever.

Looking at Tim, Fred called out to Judith, "My men here are some hungry, the little one's even shaking."

Judith saw the hand and understood what it all meant. Knowing the health nurse to be visiting Aunt Bessey at this very moment, she immediately ran Tim up the road a ways to the house.

"Aunt Bessey caught diabetes on the day of her eightieth birthday party," they said of her. "She ate too many of those bakeapple tarts and passed right out there and then while everybody was dancing."

The nurse, Marguerite also saw and understood immediately Tim did not have an ordinary infection. She directed Judith, to fetch the particular knife that had cut the boy, and to ask Fred, if he knew, for what else that knife had been used.

"I killed and butchered that seal with it yesterday, froze up the meat and cut off the flippers for that new restaurant up the road."

"Which knife did Tim just use to clean the cod?"

"This one. It's my old one I used yesterday. Not too sharp it isn't. Probably why it slipped and he cut himself."

Without saying another word Judith turned swiftly and ran back to Aunt Bessey's with the knife. As she came in Judith overheard Marguerite speaking to the emergency nurse in St. Anthony,

" ….this child, Tim Matthews, probably has contracted 'seal finger' and needs to be rushed to hospital. It sounds like some seal grease from the knife he used today has seeped into the fresh cut on his finger. He says that the cut began to throb painfully some hours ago and to me the infection appears to be moving up his arm. At the moment he is too weak to sit up by himself so his mother and I are driving him in stat."

Judith sat in the rear with her son. Trees, moose on the highway, bays and hills all flew past. "Can we go faster?" she asked.

"Not really," Marguerite answered.

Twenty minutes later Tim was wheeled into a small operating theatre. Isabelle came in a minute later. Judith knew her. "Thank you," she whispered, scarcely audible.

Since her visit last summer with Tim and his new family, Judith realized that she did not want to return home just yet. She lingered in the safety of avoidance past Christmas, and now it had turned February.

Fred tried hard to consider all the reasons why the family had drifted so far apart, particularly as to why Judith remained silent about it all.

"But has she really?" he thought out loud still holding his mug of fresh coffee. Fred long felt the distance widening between them, an estrangement that had tacitly wedged in some time years ago, very real yet unspoken. Neither knew how to approach this chasm – both were frightened because the words irretrievably spoken to one another may never be what was really meant, or wanted. So neither spoke of anything. A heavy sadness came upon Judith.

The morning hours drifted by slowly while the up-wind from the northeast weakened and the birch logs on the fire slowly reduced themselves to burning coals.

He had built the house snug against all the vagaries of northern weather, but not against the weight of withdrawal. Before Judith left for the Sault she had always been there. Over all the years he had felt the softness of her beside him. Before this strangeness between them she gave her love. She yielded and delighted in the intimacy of his caresses. He made her feel safe and she knew that he loved her.

The last night before Judith left she and Fred lay beside each other under the blankets, he, as always on his left side, and she on her back, this night staring motionless upwards towards the ceiling, feeling as if pinned by some frightening force from within her, afraid to speak aloud her intention, and terror-shaken should Fred even ask.

For the past several days Fred felt an impending dread that slowed his daily walk down to the stage. Frequently he began stumbling over aged and gnarled driftwood or familiar rocks along the landwash.

There were times when he had known fear, times when he never knew whether the sea would swallow himself, his catch, and his dory. That he understood, "but this beyond my understanding." Before tonight she had never undressed with her back to him, *so I couldn't see her*, he thought, *but why?*

The following morning, after he had left for St. Anthony, Judith sat down to write her letter.

> *Dear Fred:*
>
> *It has been a long time since we talked, I mean really talked. I feel desperately heavy and ache all over, yet so unbearably, and yes, so painfully empty. I haven't worked out how that can be, or why. But it is. I have nothing to give you — don't know how to even tell it, or…*

Her thoughts went blank. She began to sob, deep, wrenching, breathless. She crouched forward in her chair, her bent head falling against the table-top, a cup of lukewarm tea tipped over spilling onto the floor.

"Why? What has happened?"

Her words dried up. All that came were the tears, no more thoughts, no more questions. Judith crawled to the corner and lay motionless.

Amy came home the end of February. True to form, the first morning she busied herself cooking her father's favourite dish, *Cod au Gratin*. For most of the ingredients she walked over to the General Store, but the cod she found in the basement freezer. She brought up enough to make several dozen fish cakes in the afternoon. By late morning a large pot of rabbit soup, flavoured with her favourite condiments and teeming with plenty of vegetables simmered on the stove.

"How are you Dad, really?" she spoke up as they both savored the fresh bowl of soup. Amy had a way with her dad and that was to take her greatest asset, her sharp, penetrating brown eyes and look unblinking into his. When doing this, she had a way of tilting her head to the left while she waited for his answer. This usually dissolved him.

"I don't know, if truth be told," he answered slowly. "Days and nights come and go. That's all."

"Do you miss Mother?"

"Yes." His eyes averted hers as his answer sank in. He didn't usually admit to what he called weakness. Amy knew that he actually meant vulnerability. Yet Fred also knew his child: she wanted sincere, direct answers, always. On his part emotional walls and barriers tired him now. So he decided that she could have him.

Amy refilled his soup bowl.

"Mom told me that there was like a wall between us. I don't know where it came from, but it just grew and grew." Fred paused, then went on, "Just before her visit to Tim's I just felt so wretched – can't really blame her for staying there so long. Someone told me a while back, like she feels that I abandoned her long ago – left her all alone in the same house as me."

Fred hesitated, yet went on, "I still feel Judith holds against me what happened to Tim. I ordered him to stay with me after the cut happened, and would have later taken him to the back woods to fetch more of the cut logs... Just getting over another bout of pneumonia, he wasn't too strong yet.

"I was sloppy with that knife and sorry after finding out what I had done, but didn't tell him that, or your mother. He could have died."

Amy never knew her father to be so candid, and Fred never spoke to anyone about his memories.

"She loves you, Dad, and Tim didn't die or lose his finger. Dr. Isabelle fixed him up. So tell her, Dad, how sorry you are."

Amy watched her father. "Think about what Mom means about leaving her all alone. When we kids left there was only the two of you living together here in this house. We were all outside of it and away, but you were both alone together inside. Mom felt that you just shut her out – you never talked to any of us much. Just think what she felt like being so alone."

Amy continued, reached out and held his hand. "You are a fisherman and a hunter, Dad, and never left any of us hungry and cold, ever, even when the fishery died and the government shut everything down and left us with nothing. They set up empty programs to compensate us but you rose above them and squeezed out a living for us – at first there was only me and Brent."

"I am a fisherman. I left the books for you and your mother."

She thought for a moment, still watching him. "Why bring in the books, Dad?"

He backed off, gripped by a sudden fear. A lengthy silence ensued except for the kettle near boiling on the wood stove. Still she watched him. He knew she was waiting for an answer, she always did. He looked to the floor.

Fred got up without a word, turned abruptly without looking her way and walked out and towards the shed.

Yes, she had inadvertently exposed him, probably shamed him. However, Amy could not have foreseen it, but now understood something that neither he nor her mother had ever revealed. She saw the excruciating pain in his face and the tear that fell silently onto the tablecloth before he gruffly walked out. Her father suddenly knew that she saw what he and her mother had never told her.

Amy rose, walked to the window and saw him sitting on his old wood horse staring out across the ice. As she thought about it, there were, over the years, many, now obvious telltale signs, and looks that passed between her parents to which none of the children were privy. Many, she remembered, concerned magazines, homework and letters read and written, and how, when these came up her dad would frequently retreat, somewhere, usually to his skiff and stage. Amy also remembered, every time she had ever handed him a book or an assignment from school, he took it, his look fixed intently on her face, seldom at the paper offered him.

An hour passed and he had not moved. She knew that it was she herself who needed his forgiveness, she who had been so desperate to help him, yet too inexperienced to hold back.

Amy threw on her coat and his mukluks, walked out with the frozen snow crunching beneath her. She sat down beside him. Both sat quietly for some minutes.

"Dad, I am so sorry. Please forgive me."

He loved her so much and wanted to say the right words, yet could not find them. After another several minutes Fred placed his arm around her. Amy leaned her head against her father's shoulder. For the longest time they sat nestled together on the wood horse. The only sound came from the tinkling of frozen snow crystals blown softly across unspotted whiteness.

Judith flew into the St. Anthony airport three days later. As was usually the case, Fred arrived much too early. When the plane arrived he was standing in the small receiving area. Through the window he watched as she disembarked carrying only her carry-on.

He wanted her so much. Since she phoned him yesterday, his feelings rocketed him in every direction. Was she coming home to stay, or perhaps to inform him otherwise? How was he to make it different? Did she still love him, or even want him?

Since their time together on the wood horse, he and Amy talked and a new world opened for him, but this moment, this very hour meant more than talk.

Judith walked through the same open doors through which he had seen her leave months before. With this sudden remembering there suddenly came that same crushing pain of loss. He had felt then a vague feeling of apprehension, but had no words for it. She had only looked back furtively, knowing that her departure was likely final, something that he did not suspect.

Entering the lobby she saw precisely where he stood, near the very spot where she had left him before Christmas.

She stopped. Each stood alone for this moment that seemed to stretch on indefinitely. Slowly they moved, hesitantly towards the other. Just as that taut moment of time seemed transfixed, Judith made a deliberate move towards him.

"I'm so happy to be home," she whispered her tears running down his cheek.

Fred and Judith stood alone still embracing in the centre of the waiting room after everyone else had left to claim their luggage.

"I love you Fred," she whispered.

"I missed you," he said.

They walked up the bridge of the house, opened the door and were welcomed by the aroma of cooking food, soup from yesterday, caribou meat, mixed vegetables and potatoes. On the kitchen table lay a handwritten note:

Dear Mom and Dad:

-just for you, so enjoy. I'm over at Vivian's. Her father died in hospital awhile back after driving from the west coast. She's still taking it very hard. We'll be working together starting in April. Yes, I just got the job. -be back tomorrow.

Love you both,

Amy

~ ~

Vivian and Nathan married in the little white church up on the hill, three years and a day from the time Philip and Amanda had done the same. Imogen came as Vivian's maid of honour and Trish returned home from Memorial to be the bridesmaid with Jamie covering as ring bearer. This was Trish's second time home.

The first came the autumn of her first year at school, midway through her first semester. Trish's father, Gordon, a fisherman since a boy, drowned at sea. Delora pleaded with him not to go out alone that cold autumn morning.

"Just one more time before the ice," he promised.

"Over the years she'd seen him off more than three thousand mornings," Trish told Nathan before the funeral, "and he would always come home... never did last Tuesday."

A storm had come up suddenly and blew in all directions. Delora waited for him with a gnawing worry, and before nightfall Philip, with some of the men, went looking. They found his body draped over the stern. The anchor rope had tripped him and coiled around his left leg. The sea scraped and crushed him against the cliff rocks. An autopsy in St. Anthony revealed that Gordon hit his head on the gunnels and fell unconscious into the water.

"Mom is taking this very hard. She seems to have aged over the strain of these two days. She always worried some over the years, 'but never like that morning,' she told me. 'I told him not to go by his'self to Belle Isle but he assured me."

"I knows the movement of the water and the wind and where the fish goes. That's where they're at today," he said before leaving.

"Last spring, Dad and two friends went there. The catch was plentiful and they wanted to stay 'til the next day. It was calm. The bay where they fished had no landwash to land them so they anchored and Dad sat up all night to watch for ice. The ice came near morning, moving quickly. It had run together and raftered, and the floe threatened to pin and crush the dory 'gainst the rocks. Dad woke his men just in time to find a narrow break running north."

Nathan and Trish sat close together on a very old pine bench surrounded by beautiful Arctic evergreen shrubs with their bell-like flowers – her Mother's favourite.

~ ~

What about Thérèse, that girl so alone and angry? She left Nathan the morning they arrived from that ill-fated Christmas visit to the north coast. Thérèse did not return to college that semester, and Nathan never again saw her.

During their first semester together, Nathan had the impression that he and Thérèse had grown to love one another. Perhaps they had, he thought.

Yet Thérèse's reaction to his family in Newfoundland left him bewildered, and indeed remorseful over his own crippling passivity. Thérèse had suddenly, brazenly and virulently attacked Jenny – Jenny whom he loved devotedly from the earliest of times when they were both children. Nathan never experienced anyone filled to the brim with such poisonous jealousy.

Thérèse herself shuddered to remember all that transpired on that Christmas Eve, the outburst and her night walk over the hills surrounding the cove, their hasty retreat the following morning, and the long drive along the straits and inland west back to campus – two days and a night of excruciating silence.

For Thérèse, the next months until early spring remained a blur. There were times when she walked all day, and times where she lay down to sleep in some field or on some shore where all she could hear, or wanted to hear, was the sound of lapping water or the distant hum of traffic. She remained indifferent to the cold, the snow and the rain.

Thérèse relived the nightmare of her losing her child. It haunted her waking hours, and aroused her as she slept. Through these night hours she startled awake at the sound of a diving frog or the sudden early morning honking of overhead Canada Geese. Upon waking, whether in the dead of night or early morning, there it was yet again – the memories and suffocating feelings of being so deeply flawed. There were days and night when fear and the dread of uncertainty stalked her without relief.

Then there were also those encroaching practical realities. Thérèse was running low on the funds she had withdrawn months before, money that remained from her uncle's gift to her: "You hide it and use it, girl, whenever the time comes for you to leave here." Her clothing needed repair. She felt dirty and smelly, and tried to avoid sitting near anyone in any of the small restaurants she occasionally went in to eat – usually for warmth, and for those toilets and wash basins she had always taken for granted.

Thérèse was alone in the desert. She experienced this time as a barrenness and a nakedness that to her seemed endless. There were days when she felt inconsolable and despairing.

Nevertheless, a memory stirred within her, not those jarring, threatening ones but one that she now experienced with a hope of someday soon waking into newness. Passing by a church, she opened the large oak door and went in. It was early one evening, in April, she later remembered. The sanctuary appeared empty. All was quiet. The light from the crimson sunset outside lit the cross over behind the altar. Thérèse slowly walked to the front. She slid into a pew. An expectation, however very faint, rose within her. As yet she could give no substance to it, no idea what to expect – if anything really. It was so warm and in here, Thérèse finally felt safe. She slowly slouched down into the pew, lay down and fell asleep.

Thérèse stirred from a movement near to her. She quickly sat up. A nun sat beside her on the pew.

"Oh, I'm very sorry... I just fell off."

"Hello, I'm Sister Martha. Just call me 'Marty.' My friends gave me that nickname long ago and it just stuck. What's your name?"

"Thérèse."

"Well Thérèse, come on into the apartments and we'll talk over some hot chocolate, if you would like."

Again Thérèse nodded, and warmed to this Sister who everyone called just "Marty."

And again, as with Sylvia and her husband so long ago now, she talked freely while Marty just listened – to all of it. Suddenly, somewhere in her telling, Thérèse did not feel so empty, so alone. *Marty,* she thought, *just understood everything...*

"Oh how I miss Sylvia..."

"Would you like to call her?"

Thérèse remained silent, sinking into thoughts that "maybe they are too disappointed in me. They'll perhaps just tell Sister to send me away, certainly not to them."

"No, not right now. They must think that I threw myself off some gulch and my body got washed out by the tide."

"Well, in the meantime, young lady, here are some towels, soap and a washcloth, and here in this bedroom off the kitchen is your bed, and to your left is a shower – I dare say that you will really need that one," she said smiling. Marty began walking out of the kitchen.

Thérèse felt as if she were merely going through some set of motions, as if all this was actually surreal, an illusion.

"You can call her."

"Good. I'll wake you before breakfast," was the last Thérèse heard from her until morning.

Marty had placed a large orange, a sandwich and a glass of milk beside the bed. Nearly asleep, Thérèse ate half the sandwich and a few sips of the milk...

In the morning over breakfast Marty informed Thérèse that she and Sylvia had this chat, for several hours actually, "and, if it was still okay by you, Sylvia could come by around ten and take you home with her."

"Thank you. That sounds really cool. Can I ask you for something... could I borrow that *Gospel of Luke* on the table beside the bed, and that book of Newfoundland poetry by Pratt lying on top of the closet? In the hostel behind some shelved books I discovered an old volume of Pratt's Newfoundland poems. I usually woke early and began reading a bit from both...

"As a little girl in my room I would often read the "Rachel poem," as I called it, over and over."

"Did something happen in your life that draws you to it?"

"In some way it reminds me of my friend Jake, my only friend really, ever. I had him for a short while in grade seven and eight. Our desks sat next to each other. He and his father went off fishing one morning and never came back that night, lost somewhere off the southeast coast, perhaps caught in a whirlwind at sea.

"My parents didn't like him; no, they despised him. My brothers bullied him at school, particularly after they saw us holding hands. So Jake never came over to the house.

"During the nights in my room I missed him very much.

"We were all having dinner, the day they found their bodies washed up, my Mother, usually quick to sprinkle her usual venomous remarks, said, looking directly at my Dad, and realizing that I was already too upset to eat, " At least we're now rid of....

"Her cruelty had the desired effect. I dashed from the table."

"Now where has that girl run off to..." was the cutting voice that trailed away from me as I ran from the house to where the moon was full and the air was fresh from the sea just over the hill.

"That's where I ended up, sitting on 'my rock,' crying out to the sea the pain in my stomach, and by now the intractable grief that was there, endlessly on and on. I remember feeling so deserted.

"I once wrote an essay for our English course about Pratt's *Newfoundland Seamen*. Isn't it weird that some people see us here on the east coast as living on the edge of this earth, and for them it remains only one more step to fall off, into where – nothingness? Isn't their restless busyness and daily noise a distraction, itself 'nothingness?' Yet for even those fishing nearshore in their dory, let alone for those far off in deeper waters, this edge has become the very real centre of their world. I read the last verse many times over this morning – the way of life and passion, "here" in their dories, by this edge on the sea, neither urgent news from overseas, nor the plane screeching overhead unheeded on its way to Montreal or New York have the slightest relevance for them bent over their morning's catch. I love the first few lines about we Newfoundlanders sharing bread and giving shelter – that's us."

Marty watched Thérèse's face intently, praying to discern, to understand, beyond what she was saying, seeing into her inner world. Marty began to marvel at this gifted girl, having had to struggle so desperately through her desert months, nearly bereft, forgotten and hopeless, yet never alone.

"Of course – you can have both these books, just come back for a visit and we'll talk about them. I love *Luke*, my favourite Gospel."

Thérèse sat quietly, pensively, sipping a warm cup of tea, watching Marty bake those fresh pancakes while warming maple syrup in the microwave.

She continued in a near whisper, "In these last weeks I have thought more often about my situation, where was I going, what was to happen – last evening when I arrived in the church, there were three dollars and some change left for me, and that's all I had. Yet, all through these months of walking, I always had enough for a bite to eat and a warm coffee, and my boots never wore out…"

~ ~

For Thérèse the years moved on.

During the first year in her new home, Thérèse often visited Marty. An intimate bonding of trust grew in Thérèse. Their chats over lunches covered everything and anything, from literature to astronomy, from heart-aches and growing pains, to Marty's deep love for the Gospels. Never before had Thérèse felt anything resembling these new experiences. With Marty, Sylvia, her husband Ed and family she knew herself loved, and perhaps above even that in these early years, safe.

Her grades in college saw a steady increment from her first year and now into her third. There had been no contact with her parents.

Dear Mom and Dad:

It has been a very long time since we have spoken, or even written. I have been attending university and enjoying it very much, and have found out, my profs told me, that I have a gift for physics and mathematics. Because of this they have encouraged me to apply to grad school somewhere on the mainland, which I did – and this will begin for me next fall.

For a number of years now I have thought to write you a letter expressing a few things I experienced as a younger girl. I mean to say that I have begun to understand them a bit more, and have, furthermore, refused to allow many very hurtful things to dominate me.

Through many times, hours, days and months, yes even years, of my childhood, and certainly my teen years, I remember as if each day were but yesterday, spending a lot of time closed away in my bedroom, reading, perhaps day dreaming far too much. Almost the entire time I sat on my bed looking out the window and at the hills around our house, and took tremendous pleasure at the moose often crossing through our back gate. Especially one year, I remember fondly a mother and her calf, I named Mary and Martha – never did see them again, ever. I remember feeling very lonely. Knowing what they had come to mean to me over the last while, you, Father, came into the room one evening and announced with a frightening loud voice, "last weekend I shot your Martha. We're having part of her for dinner tomorrow after church." Then you turned abruptly and left the room.

I just stared at the back of you walking away – didn't know what to say. I began to tremble. There also thundered into me in that moment the realization of abandonment - my own.

For years you and Mother denied the abuse by my own brothers. I mentioned this to you before, how they stalked quietly into my room, or barged in, like you did that night, Father, and pushed me hard against the floor – of course there was no one ever at home to hear my screams. After a while I didn't bother and just lay quietly and waited for everyone to leave. But afterwards, I trembled all over, and the shame, and following this toxic shame the pain, and then I left my body just lying there, everything became as if it never happened, and then there was no more pain, no shame, no more rage, not even my body. Yes, that was abandonment – by you, by all of you. Not only that, you violated me. Looking back now and remembering the insufferable loss I felt, and I felt it all alone.

Yes, Father, that was abandonment, an insufferable loss - by you, by all of you. I felt it all alone.

Still to this day I get flashbacks, especially at night, and I curl up under the blankets, really cold and shaking, scared like I was back then; at times I will lie there and just shiver uncontrollably.

You told me to leave the house and never return – discarded, though actually, that did relieve me of so much torment, such a bondage because by this time, I had become so afraid of all four of you.

I met a lot of beautiful people through these past years, and some I hurt really badly. There was a boy – I met him at school. His name is Nathan. His family lives on the Labrador. I treated him so badly, and his family, one Christmas. I do not know what came over me, with so much anger, and striking out at people I really cared about. It wasn't really me, just something that burst out almost irrationally – part of me stood outside watching all this. That part of me became horrified. I yelled inside for me to stop but I didn't stop. Nathan has a niece, Jenny, I think, whom he loves more than anyone. I was so jealous, then malevolent and cruel to her. I am so very sorry - and the drinking after we arrived back home, it went on and on. Then I left him. I'm so sorry.

A month or two prior to that black Christmas I became pregnant. Nathan had no idea. A girlfriend from class had an abortion done just several weeks before and assured me that there is nothing to it: "they put you to sleep and that's the end of it." - she was so terribly wrong. Even though I did see a counselor from school to "prepare" me, they said, nothing would stem the agonizing ambivalence, even up to the final moment before the anesthetic hit *me: I wanted to scream, "No, No, stop!" but could not. For weeks and months after I felt like someone had ripped me open and tore away my baby. As I lay in bed, I felt so much rage. I began to drink away my sleeplessness, and oh yes, excruciating sadness and guilt- and then came our trip to his family on the Labrador. I confessed all to Marty and Sylvia – it has taken a while but I now feel clean, atoned and forgiven Marty says.*

I heard a lady from the church you now attend. When you are asked about the children, you were heard to say that there are only the two boys and that a daughter that might have once been died at term about twenty or so years ago. That, I take it is me, right? In other words, to you, Mom and Dad, I never really was?

For the longest time after I left you, years perhaps, I tried to hate you, to despise you for everything that happened. There have been a few times when it actually made me ill. Nevertheless, I have forgiven you. When I heard about your comments that I had died before birth, I walked down to the landwash, wept, and later that night I forgave you again.

I have been living with this family while attending university, and some years before actually. I have come to love them as my own, and they me, and for this I am eternally grateful.

I hope all is well with you. I will not be writing again,

Thérèse

VI

Change Islands, Newfoundland

Dennis rehabilitated very well from his illness and surgery yet remained unable to keep up with his son in the bush, or inshore fishing. He also began looking considerably older, and saddened. A significant depression settled in over him by the second day home. Naomi removed the sutures towards the end of week two, and by the second month his mood lifted.

Ron also rallied following his medivac from the island and emergency surgery. Cynthia stayed with him during these two weeks after which he was discharged with no expected complications.

On the day of Ron's admission she booked the same Bed and Breakfast as did Laura later in the week. Cynthia did not understand Laura's sudden departure that morning. The following day, she had intended to meet Laura for lunch. Laura never showed. Cynthia returned to the Bed and Breakfast. The hostess remembered Laura complaining of a migraine the evening before. No one yet knew that she had already left.

Laura had awakened in the morning before breakfast and moved about stealthily. The hostess heard nothing until a car pulled into the driveway and seconds later backed out. "It was likely a taxi.".

~ ~

A year later, Ron and Cynthia returned with the boys and settled into an old house in Goose Cove on the Northern Peninsula, a few miles south of St. Anthony.

Ron loved the thought of renovating their three-bedroom house that overlooks the North Atlantic.

For two months of this year Cynthia planned to fly on to Kingston and there resume her part-time law practice.

The very first time the boys saw an iceberg or a whale visiting the Cove, they ran into the kitchen, awestruck and excited dragging their parents over the hill and across streams and splashing through puddles to the shore.

Early in summer that first year Cynthia did fly to Kingston where she had kept her condominium. During the end of her second week she attended a dress up staff dinner held at one of her favourite Italian restaurants. The office had asked her to be the speaker for the after-dinner presentation and in this way share some thoughts about her new life "up there."

Towards the end of her presentation Cynthia intended to describe something about the icebergs as they passed along the Alley in front of their house.

> ...For years, and more so recently, this area off shore has become
> a crowded corridor for passing icebergs. By tides and wind some
> of these silent mountains of ice are driven helplessly into shallow
> water and remain grounded. Eventually they may collapse in a
> thunderous crack and rumble resounding across the cove and into

the hills around. In so doing the berg breaks into growlers and hundreds of bergy-bits. This in turn frees the larger parent iceberg from off its mooring on the ocean floor to once again join the cold Labrador current, bearing him and pressing him relentlessly south.

As we all settled into our home and community, the boys occasionally went out in their boat to collect a few tiny bergy-bits left floating as a means to add ten thousand year-old freshwater ice fragments to our drinking water.

For this evening's dinner she sat beside one of the guests, a young journalist, activist and writer for Inuit concerns and Nature Conservancy issues in Nunavut. Erik was a tall man, blonde, of fair complexion and penetrating eyes, perhaps Danish, she thought – he was. His obvious enthusiasm for the cause of saving the Arctic from pollution and further encroachment dominated much of the conversation. With sparkling eyes, insight and wit, Erik's tales from the north captivated everyone around the table, that is until he began to focus primarily on Cynthia. From that point on there were just the two of them.

"Specifically, what have you been involved with recently?" she asked, at first rather self consciously.

"The council in Grise Fjord has requested me to look into climate change's effect on polar bear survival on Ellesmere Island. It's a very serious issue for the Inuit living there. People down here are usually dismissive about that – most really make a point of not knowing anything about it. They make opinions nevertheless, most of them intentionally misleading."

After some time Erik abruptly changed the subject. "I first saw you in the office last week while visiting a close friend, Steve. He actually invited me to come tonight, saying that I might find it very interesting."

"Was he right?"

"Yes. When I asked him about you, Steve said that you had, only this Spring, sold your house and moved into a village in northern Newfoundland, Goose Cove is it?"

"Yes. I've returned to work for several months to keep the bread and salmon on the table, so to speak. For much of the year, we all bake our own bread." Cynthia chuckled a bit nervously.

"And what is life like in Goose Cove?"

"It's beautiful, and peaceful. In the past, years ago, it was a French sealing and fishing outpost." She hesitated. "What do you want to know, about the people?"

"That is a good start." Erik's eyes followed her every movement as she spoke, looking for her every subtle gesture.

"Well, they are genuine, warm, spontaneous. They took us in as if we had just returned from vacation and had always been part of them. The first Saturday we were in the Cove, they invited us next door – about twenty people had crowded into the kitchen and brought out the fiddles and accordions – what a party!"

He told her about the Inuit in the north.

She in turn now looked at him closely, a bit on guard by her own intense feelings towards this man whom she had just met. She was drawn to him, attracted by the movement of his eyes as he looked at her, his lips as he spoke, his hands as they clasped the wine glass, and his slight strabismus that she found very attractive. She listened, fascinated, her own eyes fastened on his.

On Monday she went to the office expecting to see him walk in all morning. By late afternoon Erik still had not come. He never came the following day or the next.

Thursday near closing time, very discouraged and wondering aloud to herself all manner of inanities, she asked Steve, "Have you heard at all from Erik, the journalist. He came to dinner last Saturday?"

"Yes. He flew to Resolute on Devon Island for a conference, Sunday morning I believe – a last minute thing. He should be back this weekend."

Once back in the office she checked her e-mails – yes, Erik had written apologizing for leaving without so much as a good bye. She e-mailed back: *Why should you apologize for anything? Just today we were all speaking about what you've been up to. I hope your conference was what you had hoped it to be.*

The evening Erik returned from the north, they went dining. This time there were red roses that she placed on her desk by the window, and now at the restaurant she knew so well, candles and carnations.

Before the entrée arrived he reached over and she brought her hand across the table to touch his.

"I've fallen in love with you. It's never happened to me before. At the environmental meetings this week it was as if I had an attention deficit – all I thought about was you."

His eyes held hers. Cynthia felt incredible, relieved by his profession of love and wanted desperately to say something that made sense yet all seemed muddled: "that's so nice." Heat rushed to her face. She became giddy and at the same time painfully embarrassed.

"Do you really want to live in Newfoundland?" his voice almost pleading. "Here you have it made. Besides, I put your name in the minutes this week recommending you for a position as representing attorney for the council in Pangnirtung, eastern Baffin Island."

He leaned forward to kiss her hand. Cynthia now tingling with desire rose to meet him as he crossed the table for a long kiss that brought smiles from their corner of the dining room.

Dinner finished; Erik took her onto the dance floor. A jazz group from Quebec had begun a slow waltz.

Hesitatingly she moved closer until his arms held her tightly. She felt weak. She seemed to collapse into him. They kissed long and soft while moving slowly as one to the beat of the band. Midway through the following dance number she slipped away from him and sat down.

"I'm not ready for this," she exclaimed breathlessly. "Would you please take me home?" She spoke it and trembled.

When they arrived back at the condo, Cynthia tore herself away and left him standing outside the door. As the door closed she leaned against it for a long while, unable to think, her feelings tumbling around like a teenage girl. At one moment she wanted to open the door and call Erik back, at another she noticed the call light on. There was a message.

Ron called to inform her that Tommy had tripped over some rocks covered with some sort of seaweed and fractured his ankle, and then fell headlong into the water. An e-mail also waited for her:

> ...*What made it more painful was when he hobbled back home on it. I immediately took the boys into St. Anthony where a 'Doctor Isabelle', as everybody calls her, ordered x-rays and a cast. Tommy's okay. He'll still have the cast on when you come home. Mrs. Adams from next door brought over some hot soup. She assured Tommy that it would heal everything. We miss you.*

Ron sent an e-mail the day before, which she had not yet opened:

> It's a good thing that I brought all my tools up here… got two
> referrals in the last few days. A fellow from up the coast wants me
> to renovate his house, and another, Jim from around the corner a
> bit, asked me this morning if I was up for hire for the same thing.
> I did finish putting in the hardwood floor this week. It's all ready
> for you to come home.

"Oh goodness, what is happening? What am I doing here? Why am I coming back here?" Cynthia thought again aloud, "I'm so alone here. I've known the busyness and noise of this place for years. I once lived it, loved it but today it crowds in on me and suffocates me."

Her feelings turned to anger, angry with Erik for his impositions and certainties.

"I allowed myself to be carried into his attraction for me, and mine for him. I want no part of it. I'm going home, Friday. My son has a broken foot."

She laughed at her own statement: a simple broken foot will resolve this life-altering mess.

She sat alone on the sofa, turned to her CD of Verdi's opera *La Traviata*, based on a tragic story by the great French author, Alexandre Dumas. It is a story of a courtesan who, having only months to live, falls in love with an ardent suitor. Violetta has erected a wall around herself for protection, yet she ultimately yields to him. There ensues a tumultuous, passionate relationship set to the most glorious music. The story's trajectory over four acts, however, ends in consumption, heartache and death.

Cynthia sat up late listening, and reflecting on that story before eventually falling asleep.

In the morning while at work she called her realtor, listed her condo for sale and handed Steve her resignation.

"Why? ," he asked.

"Why?" she answered incredulously, "because my son has a broken foot."

Erik placed a bid in for the condo, immediately purchased it and left Cynthia a note: *If you're not coming to me, at least I have your condo. I feel you here and will wait here for you to eventually come...*

Cynthia phoned him: "I am not coming back, ever. I have a husband and two children. I love the three of them more than anything else... or anyone. Goose Cove *is* my home."

"Nevertheless, I will wait here," he answered.

The boys were eager to show Cynthia their trophies: Tommy, his cast already autographed by his pals, and Matthew, a bouquet of Blue Flag Iris' he had picked from the flower-covered pathway running along the stream out back.

Ron drove up to the airport some ten minutes before Cynthia's Twin Otter landed. As she walked into the airport, the children ran up to her excitedly.

Ron held back. Cynthia looked up from the boys. For a long moment her eyes met his and spoke an intimate, silent message she and he knew so well. She smiled and walked into his arms, "I love you," Cynthia whispered. Tears of happiness filled her eyes, running down her cheeks. "I'm home," she continued.

In another month the house became fully renovated and Ron began working up the coast a short ways. One morning, the Friday before Thanksgiving, Cynthia received an e-mail from Steve:

> *...Would you consider working part time from home? You need not ever come down. A client from last year requested that you personally help him finish up some business. I would really appreciate having you on board for some of these scattered cases.*
>
> *By the way, do you remember Erik? From a month after he purchased your condo, Agatha moved in with him, a girl he had met last year in Ottawa. They've been quite a serious item for quite a while. We had them over for dinner last week – very nice girl. She teaches secondary school geography and loves their new condo. How is your son's foot?*

Cynthia read to the end, sat quietly looking out to sea. Her response was terse:

Just this once — no more.

~ ~

And Arnold - he began teaching at Memorial University last year. This year it became a permanent position allowing him a substantial grant, which in turn enabled him to carry on research field trips in the Limestone Barrens outside Raleigh.

These field trips with his students opened opportunities for him to visit his family, Amanda, Philip, Mark and a new granddaughter, Suzanne. He came home the weekend of Amanda's bride-in feast, a many-generations-old custom when Newfoundlanders came together to celebrate this new birth.

Arnold purchased a condominium within a short walk from Cape Spear on the Avalon. At times he looked back over those difficult years of despondency and separation but it was that reunion on the river's edge that replayed over and over, a gift of grace and healing.

Amanda adored her dad and she too remembered that uncertain walk over to the picnic table that morning by the river. Time seemed to stand still for those few seconds, yet Amanda's walk came to symbolize for her a release, the beginnings of her ongoing healing from her mother's vitriolic assaults and those vile encroachments from Roger.

VII

Cape Bauld Lighthouse, Quirpon, Newfoundland

And so the seasons passed.

Two pristine icebergs were the first to appear in late winter, jammed into an icepack moving south along the Alley. The first was gilded by a sculpted tower spiraling skyward, the other marked by luminous, shimmering fissures — two beautiful masterpieces vulnerable amidst stream currents carrying them along the coast past St. Anthony, Englee, Fogo and Twillingate.

In spring and early summer these bergs attracted pods of orcas and humpbacks, and herds of seal, all of them feeding off the fresh abundance of food stirred up by these passing bergs.

However, from then until late September, the weather grew coarse and erratic. Thrashing seas in summer altered shorelines. Rafted ice and growlers threatened fishermen in their dories.

The cold onset of winter came early.

Isabelle left Ship Cove one early morning in mid-November. Susan and Martin had spent their first Autumn in their newly renovated house, and now it was winter.

These had been wonderful days of being together, hiking, reading and, as she was fond to say, just hanging out. The morning Isabelle left, a light snow covered the tuckamore groves, and a stillness she had come to love permeated the land. Before getting into her car, she listened to the restless groaning as the sea heaved beneath the compacting saltwater ice and beyond. She knew from her life on the coast that this stinging, cold upwind coming in from the sea looked ahead to a gathering storm. She was right. By mid-day a screecher would shut down the road and near everything in its path for days ahead.

Driving home to St. Anthony and rounding a curve she drove up to five moose standing still across the now frozen, snow covered road ahead of her. The adults, four cows and a bull appeared, as is often the case, somewhat stunned, gazing at the intruder. A calf lingered in the gulley beside her.

She knew it was best to wait them out. They would decide the time to move on. After five minutes of gazing and very little thought, one moved, then all five followed, trotting off along a path and disappearing into the woods to her right. The young calf faltered in the snow, struggling to keep pace.

Another kilometer, and another moose, a cow moving quite swiftly alongside the road. Isabelle tried to gauge her movements, knowing how erratic and unpredictable she could become. Suddenly the moose turned left, directly towards Isabelle's car. Isabelle's leg lunged for the brake. The car slid and hit the moose, forcing itself between her legs, her upper body smashed through the windshield, crushing the panel, her eyes now staring through the steering, her breathing hot and gurgling. Steam rising from the radiator mixed with the blood from the animal spraying across Isabelle's face. The car had skidded onto its side and down the shallow gulley. Isabelle was thrown onto the side of the pavement. Her own blood streamed down her temple and into her eyes.

Only just able to see, Isabelle clawed her way back into the car, found her cell phone and pressed the quick dial.

At the hospital, the girl on switchboard heard a faint beep – being in a valley surrounded by hills, Isabelle's voice did not transmit. She knew herself bleeding profusely, feeling faint, her nausea overwhelming…

"André…," she whispered, "André."

She lost consciousness.

Nevertheless at the switchboard, the "bleep" continued, gradually fainter and fainter. Then, it fell silent.

The phone's brief contact did leave her number.

The nurse on call phoned Martin.

Martin knew from years experience and vigilance what this meant. He grabbed blankets, Susan her medic's kit. As they both ran for the skidoo and komatik, the snow began to pile up around their bridge. The wind came in blustery from the northeast.

Martin knew the road now visible only in short stretches and these were quickly filled in.

Susan felt the fear.

Martin sped ahead full throttle. He risked no shortcuts. Freshly fallen snow, deep and soft could catch him unawares, so he followed the road.

Martin fought with all his nerve and strength, driving his skidoo and sled forward, attacking against the drifting snow. Susan sat on the seat behind him, holding onto his body, feeling his every strain.

An eternity of time seemed to pass. As yet he saw nothing.

Plowing over the crest of a hill, they spotted a light, blinking, barely perceptible through the screeching wind and snow.

Martin was the first to see her. Isabelle had slipped from the car to where she now lay over the still warm body of the moose. She was still clutching the cell phone.

Susan quickly crawled over to her friend. Isabelle was alive. She had seemingly lost much blood. Her right radius was broken and possibly several ribs fractured. Susan removed some clotted hair around the injury and quickly ascertained an open scalp wound. Much of the bleeding had come from this, although as yet, she was anxious about internal bleeding. She gently removed clotted hair from around the injury and reached into her medical kit she always carried with her...

Because of the high hills and dense rock in the area Martin did not know if his own cell phone would connect. It did. He made an urgent call into St. Anthony. They had already traced Isabelle's location by her phone's "bleeps."

Already fearing the worst, an ambulance had been dispatched, specially equipped for such a call in an imperiled time as this.

In hospital for the first day, Isabelle drifted in and out of sleep and confusion. Her arm was fractured, as were several ribs.

Susan's fear of internal bleeding was relieved although Isabelle had had a significant loss of blood from the head wound around the time of the collision. Beside this, having lain unconscious and immobile for some time, Susan had seen signs of frostbite and beginning the onset of hypothermia.

At the scene, she and Martin had wrapped her in blankets and when the ambulance came Susan accompanied Isabelle, still unconscious, to the hospital.

While Martin returned home, Susan had sat with Isabelle in the ambulance and remained beside her all that day and the next. Quite often through that first day Isabelle whispered André's name, a name Susan had never heard from her over the years since they first met.

Gradually, the days passed. Isabelle's radial fracture was set. She suffered no residual effects from the frostbite or head injury and within five days, and a week before Christmas, Isabelle was discharged on condition that she not return to work for a month.

The storm that had brought Isabelle into hospital left her house buried. Nevertheless, by the time of her discharge, the neighbours had shoveled the house free of snow. During the three day storm the wind had come with such force that the furnace "blew out," as Marg next door told it, "and de folks shoveled the snow and unfroze dem pipes for you."

~ ~

Her close friends loved her. Whether as an intimate friend or trusted physician, Isabelle was warm, dedicated and intelligent. Her genuineness and ready smile made her all the more attractive. Isabelle came to this coast in the hope of finding fulfillment in her work, and a place to settle. She found it.

Nevertheless they all, Susan, Martin, Philip and Amanda, perceived a sadness, something as yet unspoken to any of them, perhaps hinted at only to Susan.

She would wander off by herself – these were her times. Her friends understood and afforded Isabelle the space.

Those snow bound days she and Susan first spent together was the time Isabelle had flown to Nain to escort the lady suffering from a heart attack. During those days, Isabelle told Susan that she had been a keen soccer player and fan, and on the way to becoming an accomplished pianist. Music was initially her major at university until she inadvertently paged through her older brother, Gerald's, cardiac textbook, "at least most of the thirteen-hundred pages."

"I was hooked," she told Susan. "Shortly thereafter I read the biography of Dr. Grenfell – that was it. I knew then and there where my calling lay, and vowed to become a physician."

Isabelle's strength had not fully returned by Christmas. She came to Ship Cove to join with Martin and Susan on their first holiday in their new home. While Martin fell asleep on the sofa, the girls put on their mukluks and parkas, walked over the hill, down the droke lined on either side with tuckamores, and into Cape Onion.

The land and sea were crystal white. All was flat calm as the warm sun sparkled off a nearby Labrador ice island that had drifted late into the Alley at the time the ice set fast in the bay.

They came to the bench looking over the bay. The old heritage inn behind them and the distant Great Sacred Islands ahead appeared as if frozen in time. All was hushed. The only occasional sound came from the powerful groanings of the sea, closed in under the ice.

Through her sunglasses Isabelle gazed far out to sea.

"Isabelle," Susan broke in, "do you miss him?"

Isabelle sat silent for a minute, then shook her head. "Yes. Andre."

"I met him during my fourth year. We fell madly in love. He was ahead of me by three years, and by then a senior in a pediatric residency. Two years went by. We worked and studied apart most days. Whoever came home first made dinner. The other cleaned up. We tried hard to discipline ourselves and never leave a dirty kitchen. However, my touch left him trembling. His touch…well let me put it this way…he carried me over the threshold. Bedtimes were intensely passionate.

"We attended concerts together and in my spare time I played the piano again. I even played an all Chopin recital for a fund-raiser that included some works I had taken a year to relearn.

"André asked me to marry him after residency. I had three more years to go.

"Just before André left one morning, right by the kitchen door, he collapsed. With my cell phone in one hand I rushed to where he fell, examined him quickly and suspected an intracerebral hemorrhage. I called 911. He hadn't complained that morning of headache or nausea, not even dizziness, you know those symptoms that show something like that impending.

"Before the ambulance arrived, André was dead. When the paramedics arrived they found me slumped down on the floor with his head in my lap.

"His parents live in Germany, that's where André was born. My parents died some years before. My brother flew in to be with me.

"André's funeral was in the stone church on campus. The priest was wonderful, and very insightful. I leaned on him for a while, you know, and his wife invited me over for dinners. I never told Amanda but they were the same people that helped her through that terrible abuse with her mother and stepfather… I've never before spoken to anyone about André…

"Soon my residency exams were only a year away. For the first while following André's death they seemed unreal. I couldn't look ahead to them… really pushed myself over the hump… anyway I did pass and finished quite well… and here I am. I've probably locked myself down a bit and not really resolved the grief…

Before Andre, there was Tom, an overbearing and shallow chap - so very different. He was a lawyer studying to be an architect. And me, I was a medical student. Right from the beginning he planned out our lives. With me at his side, he repeated often, "we will make loads of money and go places, that you (*that is me*) have never dreamed of."

"I told him that being a medical missionary somewhere, perhaps in Africa or Canada's north, would satisfy me.

"When he realized that I was serious, Tom's way of speaking to me became, at least far too often, abrasive. He accused me of depriving him, "no both of us," he added, of a great future, "and with all our money we will likely own a beach house in Cape Cod. With both of our incomes put together we could afford our children, if we had any, a first rate Nanny.

"Tom began to ridicule my faith, then despise it, claiming that he didn't have time for God, 'even if there is one.'

"He became distant. There was nothing left between us and we just fell apart. These deep differences between us became two yawning chasms that could never be breached. I accepted this long before him.

"Yes, I miss André. I did love him... I still do actually."

The lustre of the ice in the harbour began to dim as the girls arrived back in the house. Martin awoke.

Later, sitting around the yule tree Martin and Susan opened their gift from Isabelle, her first work, published just before Easter – a set of twenty-two short stories and poetry, most of which take place in the Shetlands of northern Scotland, her birthplace.

Isabelle opened her gift box. In it were two Inuit carvings, the first a loon and the other an Inuksuk, by Martin's father in Baker Lake.

Martin then requested Isabelle to read St. Luke's timeless telling of the Incarnation. Grace and thanksgiving said, Susan brought out Christmas dinner and on the occasion of this special homecoming Martin uncorked the chilled wine he had saved since summer.

As the fire crackled in the background, from the window the early moon was seen reflecting on the Labrador Sea-ice as it lay infrangible in glacial stillness. And so they spent their early evening together, conversing easily about things past and dreams that each yet hoped for.

Since the mid-eighteen hundreds a tradition had built up in the Cove for a community gathering in St. Stephen's Church hall in the evening of Christmas day. The invitation came as a personal welcome to Susan, Martin and Isabelle by Mrs. Noseworthy in early December. All three were already well known by all of the families living in and around the Cove.

Martin was known as the pilot for the "mission," Susan as the nurse from Labrador, and Isabelle the doctor who had already carried many of the children through various afflictions and crises, most often appendicitis, fractures and childbirth.

They walked in just ahead of several families carrying the accordions and fiddles. Isabelle and Susan brought in three freshly baked strawberry pies nearly tripping over some of the children dancing excitedly around them, or nibbling on the warm, fresh partridgeberry muffins already on the serving table.

By the time they walked home the moon no longer mirrored over the crystal sea ice and the air, though always fresh and clean, had become biting cold. The embers of the fire left untended from dinner quickly caught into the wood Martin now laid onto it.

No one spoke. All three, exhausted from the dancing and singing, yielded to the silence of the room. There were very few words to describe their thankfulness to these neighbours, a genuine group of folk who could never have done more to make them feel affirmed and welcome, here in this Cove, on the northern shores of this land their home.

~ ~

Dear Mother:

We hope this letter finds you well. Following an unseasonably coarse summer and fall here on the coast, winter set in early this year. Looking out our window, as I write, a tight field of ice stretches well beyond the Sacred Islands and as far out to sea as anyone can see. In calm sunny mornings like today it all looks so spectacular.

The real purpose of this letter is to inform you that I am pregnant, four months actually. It's going to be a July baby - "a barn'd Newfoundlander," as we say here. This will be our first child. When the expected time arrives I would really like you to come and stay with me a bit.

Berries, Tickles and Saltwater Ice

You have not answered any of my letters. None of them were returned so you must receive them. Your telephone number remains unlisted. Have I been simply excluded from your life? Please reconsider, please come; this is your first grandchild.

A month before Christmas, Isabelle was seriously hurt in a car accident. She had just left our place early to avoid a northerner about to blow in. A small herd of moose wandered onto the road. One turned abruptly ahead of her. She hit him hard.

Before Isabelle lost consciousness she just managed to activate her cell phone. The hospital switchboard picked it up as a faint signal. Martin sensed that something had gone terribly wrong so we sped down the road in the snowmobile. When we arrived on the scene Isabelle had been knocked unconscious and was bleeding. Because of the weather and temperature hypothermia became an immediate problem.

The moose was dead, and Isabelle's car totaled. He had crashed through the windshield. An ambulance from Raleigh arrived just ahead of the road closing over. I remained with her as much as possible while in hospital. On discharge she recuperated at our place. We all spent a wonderful Christmas together.

As I have very likely mentioned earlier, your friends Ron and Cynthia pulled up their roots in Kingston, sold almost everything they owned and moved here with the boys last year. He renovated an old house in Goose Cove – that is where they live, and Cynthia works part-time for the hospital, something in the legal/ business end of things.

Love, Susan

The winter passed. A cool, brief spring yielded to a warmer summer, far more moderate than the year before.

Yet as the months had passed Susan began to know within herself, her mother dismissed her– "Was that it?"

"Perhaps there is no word," she whispered to herself, "so it's best not to think of any."

One afternoon, several weeks before term, she and Isabelle met for lunch at the Lighthouse.

"For years I have felt this coming. I always tried to shove it away, and I did, mostly. After a long pause Susan continued. "However, looking back over the years, I see how all this slowly piled up. I remember example after example, and now here it is. I can face it now, the "why?" of Mother's reactions all along, what she meant beneath it all. And now her feeling is more than ever, "if you don't play it my way and come 'home,' I won't play at all."

"I know that over the years, you have genuinely tried to reach out to your Mom but she has long ago chosen to control you and cannot, furthermore, face that you have accomplished terrific things, and a wonderful life has come together for you here - and all that beyond anything she herself could ever think. Remember, Laura's choices are not your fault."

The friends sat quietly on a bench, hand in hand, looking seaward at the incoming fog. They watched as a one-lunger passed by beneath them and headed towards the leeside of a small island of massive rock. It was calmer in there and the lone fisherman hauled up his net. There were only a few fish but what he caught, he scooped up, sunk his gear back into the water, turned around and headed home.

"Let's walk up to the Lighthouse for another mug of tea," Susan suggested tentatively, jarring, so to speak, the silence between them.

Susan's time came. Laura did not come. To her silence Susan added not a word.

Liliana was born July 16th, full term at five pounds, eight ounces. A sister Jacqueline followed in three years less a day, and a brother Alain two years later.

About the Author

Reg Faust was born "on the mainland," lived with his family in St. Anthony, Newfoundland, and worked as a northern nurse and clinical social worker with the International Grenfell Association of Newfoundland and Labrador. He has earned and received degrees from a number of universities including Memorial University of Newfoundland. This story brings together a few of the experiences of those years and reflect the lives of some of the people who live on the coast and a nurse who came to love them, the land and the sea that binds them.

Reg is presently assisting his wife, Mary Jane, while she writes a book, WHILE YOU WERE AWAY, the true story of the parental abduction of children, namely her own, four children who were suddenly stolen one Friday on their way to school, and withheld as captives, "somewhere" in the southern United States by their father. For eight and a half years, Mary Jane endured the unknown - no one could find the children and they, in turn were too terrified to call home. She did not know what they had been told about their Mother, and they in turn did not know anything but what they had been told by their Father. For this account, Reg has given relevant clinical and research insights into this pervasive and destructive violation. This is a story of excruciating pain, indomitable courage and exultant faith.

CPSIA information can be obtained at www.ICGtesting.com
Printed in the USA
LVOW06s2241130813

347718LV00001B/4/P